Hey!
Look What Others Are Saying!

D1430305

"*Hey! I'm the Manager...* Is a fascinating and fresh look at management theory and application. It is filled with case studies, wisdom-filled insight and interesting real life scenarios. This is a book you will want to read to take your management to the next level!"

— **Chris Widener**
author of *The Art of Influence: Persuading Others Begins with You*,
www.ChrisWidener.com

"Steve Farner has produced a comprehensive (yet very practical) guide for managers and employees alike. This book is filled with tips that you can put to work right away!"

—**Tom Rath**
New York Times best-selling author of *How Full Is Your Bucket? Positive Strategies for Work and Life* and *Vital Friends: The People You Can't Afford to Live Without*

"*Hey!* What a great guide for everyday management of people at all levels and types of organizations. Steve Farner's 'story' is a unique blend of insightful personal examples and proven academic research results.

This engaging, readable book will help both students and managers bridge the gap between theory and effective, not necessarily common sense, practices of managing the most complex, but important, part of their job – their people."

— **Fred Luthans**
Distinguished Professor, University of Nebraska,
author of *Organizational Behavior* (11 Editions)
and *Psychological Capital: Developing the Human Competitive Edge*

I'm the Manager...
Why Aren't You Listening to Me?

A Field Guide for Managing People

HEY!

I'm the Manager...
Why Aren't You Listening to Me?

A Field Guide for Managing People

Steve Farner, Ph.D.

FARNER GROUP

Omaha, Nebraska

ISBN10: 0-9798320-0-4
ISBN13: 978-0-9798320-0-0
Library of Congress Control Number: 2008931935
Cataloging in Publication Data on file with publisher.

Farner Group
P.O. Box 642313
Omaha, NE 68164
www.SteveFarner.com

Editorial Services: Emily Redinbaugh
Book Design: Gary James Withrow
Production, Distribution, and Marketing: Concierge Marketing Inc.

Printed in the United States of America
10 9 8 7 6 5 4 3 2 1

Contents

Introduction

I grew up and worked in our family's candy and grocery wholesale business. That's where most of my early management experience came from. I worked in the business every summer from 14 years of age through college.

Through that lens, managing people looked so easy. It seemed to be simply a matter of telling people what to do and then making sure they did it. This flawed, simplistic view of how to manage was prevalent all through my undergraduate years as a business student at Iowa State University. In fact, I got a D+ in my first management course because I rarely went to class! I honestly did not think that I would use the material and that managing people was simply "common sense."

After graduating, I transferred to a branch location in our family business near Omaha, Nebraska. Having worked under my father for the previous seven years, I thought his system of simply telling people what to do seemed so simple and yet so effective. What I, of course, didn't know was that this was not how he really did things. I was not around when he had to fire people. I was not in on the heated meetings, the restructurings, the job interviews, the visits by his boss (he was always just Grandpa to me), the promotions, demotions, or the time he caught what he thought was a loyal employee stealing from him.

So I approached my first management job assuming the people side of managing was going to be relatively easy. I understood quite well the technical side of the distribution business and had a business degree but viewed *the most important part* as common sense.

After several years of managing, I returned to graduate school. It was quite a discovery to find out that many of the areas in which I was struggling were centerpiece management topics. That is when I finally realized that an organization could really be transformed through proper management and leadership.

I have talked to thousands of practicing managers in my management courses and training seminars over the last few years. I'm struck by the fact that most of us experience similar problems when working with or managing people. The troubling stories people tell about their boss, the communication problems that they experience in their organization, or their last performance appraisal that they didn't like are universal across all different types of people, different levels of management, and in all industries.

Many of the managers in the trenches who are making decisions, hiring people, solving conflict, and conducting performance appraisals are often left to figure out how to do these things on their own. The traditional management paradigm views managing people as common sense as opposed to the complex science that it really is. This common sense approach may have worked with previous generations of managers, but today's environment has become too complex just to promote individuals and hope they can learn how to manage the people part of the job.

The previous generation had more of what I have termed *working managers*. A working manager is one who only manages on a part-time basis, with the majority of their time spent in the trenches. Examples include sales managers who spend a majority of their time actually selling, fast-food restaurant managers working the grill, or first-line supervisors who fill in when people get sick.

This is in part out of necessity because not every position requires a full-time manager. But it also is a root cause of why many organizations are managed poorly. It is because managing is often viewed as an afterthought or something to do when the "real" work is done.

Consider how most other fields in business have defined a set of knowledge that one must have in order to practice. You turn your money over to a "Certified Financial Planner (CFP)." Your accountant has a "Certified Public Accountant (CPA)" designation. You wouldn't see a lawyer who decided that law school was just common sense, so she skipped it, or an airline pilot who just had a knack for airplanes, so he never took flying lessons. However, organizations are often managed by individuals who may have talent but lack the tools or the training to effectively do their jobs.

This is further complicated by the fact that many management programs *appear* to be common sense but are in fact quite complex in the implementation. The typical things that we call "management fads that failed" are oftentimes good programs that were not implemented correctly.

How can you argue with quality management, with goal setting, with management by objectives, empowerment, self-managed teams, or pay for performance? I'd wager that if these programs left a sour taste in your mouth, it could be attributed to poor implementation by the organization. Maybe your manager told you to "do quality better" but gave you no resources. Maybe you set goals correctly but received zero feedback on them. Maybe you were "empowered" but had your boss watching your every move.

Part-time, working managers are often not equipped to give serious attention to the critical functions of management. They tend to rush through things such as performance appraisals because "customers are coming" and wonder why employees think they don't get quality feedback. They may have an "open door policy" but at the same time tell people not to bring problems, only solutions. They may tell customer service representatives to answer 20 phone calls per hour but also to make sure they spend quality time on the phone with the customers. They could be so short staffed that they don't have time to conduct quality job interviews and end up hiring the wrong person, then they wonder why turnover is so high.

The stories I tell throughout the book are true, but the names and details have been changed. After going back through the stories, it did occur to me that I may have been too hard on myself by telling mostly about my negative experiences as a manager. However, I have found that the best way to illustrate management concepts is through real-life examples. This is how I lead my classes and seminars, and I also believe that the best learning experiences happen when things don't quite go our way. I hope you will find this approach both entertaining and useful.

Steve Farner

1

Perception and the Myth of Communication Problems

"I didn't say that! Why aren't you listening?"

I used to really like quarterly manager meetings. I can remember my very first one. We were in the old warehouse conference room, complete with brown paneling across every wall. The room was packed full of people, and it was really hot and smoky. I didn't care; I was a manager now!

Relevant issues were brought up during that meeting. Accounts receivables were way too high. We used to allow our best customers 30-day credit terms, but now have required payment in seven days in order to improve cash flow. Most managers had made little progress in converting their accounts to the seven-day terms. Sales managers in the larger markets proposed a new pricing structure for candy. They said our prices were too high, and they were having trouble competing. Branch managers also discussed how the buyers, who were located at headquarters, didn't seem to communicate with them. One example was a shipment of candy that was delayed 30 days, but the branches did not know about the delay.

The discussion then turned toward developing a better system to recover the plastic totes in which products were delivered to stores. Many customers were not returning them, probably because they were the perfect size for storing items at home. Various options were discussed, including a deposit on the totes, tracking them on the computer, making the delivery drivers responsible for the totes, or simply raising prices to cover the costs.

Seven years later, about the only thing that had changed about these meetings was that we were in a larger conference room. Yes, we had grown the business significantly; our accounts receivables were better; and our future growth plans were right on schedule. Oddly however, the content of those meetings was eerily similar to the meetings I went to seven years ago. For example, accounts receivables, although better, were still way too high. And the president of the organization said that he was not communicating very well the importance of reducing the dollar amount that we were carrying on the books.

We then discussed growing sales in our larger markets. One sales manager complained that our prices were too high, and said he would be going after new customers by offering them 30 days to pay their bills. I thought it was rather humorous, given our president's speech not even five minutes ago about receivables being too high! The president did not see the humor. It seemed as if his latest speech didn't solve the "communication problem" around the receivables issue, at least for this sales manager.

After another branch manager complained about the buyers' lack of communication, the discussion shifted back toward the cost of the lost totes again. The common theme was communication, and I remember thinking that we all needed to go to a communication seminar. Our president couldn't communicate the importance of reducing receivables, managers couldn't communicate with the buyers, salespeople couldn't communicate the importance of reducing our prices in larger markets, and the warehouse foreman couldn't express properly how much this tote issue was costing the organization. Couldn't we all just communicate better?

Fast forward 10 more years: I'm in a strategic planning meeting at the university where I teach. The consensus is that the main issue that could really hamper our growth and our profitability is, well, a "lack of communication." Marketing hasn't informed customer service when advertising has run; hence they are experiencing high call volumes, which they weren't prepared for. Professors are supposed to complete a form when students don't attend class, but they don't know where to find the form, and the department heads are finding out about major decisions after they happen.

All of this is eerily similar. The only difference between today's meeting and my former meetings at the family business is that we didn't talk about returning missing totes. So what did we do? We formed a committee to study the problems. The committee determined that the root source of the problem is, yes, communication!

Communication: A Shallow Solution for Deep Issues

Both of these organizations are adept at what they do and have positioned themselves to be market leaders in their respective industries. The point is twofold. First, most organizations face the same issues. They get repackaged a bit, but basically all are facing the same things. This is because the common denominator in all organizations is people. Yes, technology is different in different industries, and people do different things, but it all involves people, and managing them makes for some interesting dilemmas.

Second, too many organizations package their problems and issues as "communication problems," which can delay solving problems and moving forward. In fact, I really can't stand to see the words *communication problem* in an analysis of what is wrong with a given organization. I have even barred my MBA students from having the words in their vocabulary, and they know that if they diagnose a case study in this fashion, they will lose points.

You see, every problem that exists in society can be traced back to some sort of communication problem. Even an argument with my wife can end if I simply throw up my hands and say, "I just can't communicate with you!" Saddam Hussein didn't really take our threats seriously because we couldn't find the right words to communicate our true intentions. I couldn't communicate very well with the police officer, so he gave me a ticket instead of a warning, and, of course, students that do poorly on exams do so because the professor didn't communicate with them well enough in regard to what was going to be on the test. I'm not denying that communication problems exist; it's just that framing the situation in a communication context hampers our efforts in solving problems.

One of my favorite case studies involves a manager who has determined that several departments are not working well together, so he calls a 6:00 Monday morning meeting in order to get them to communicate better. The meeting goes well, so the manager says as long as things continue to run smoothly, they don't have to continue the 6:00 a.m. meetings. The departments continue to work well together in the following weeks.

Many of my students conclude that the case illustrates the value of meetings in fostering communication. While this may be true to some degree, the real reason that the meeting solved the problem is that they now know that if they don't work together, they will be meeting again at an incredibly early and inconvenient hour, so they go to great lengths to avoid this punishment. Is this communication? Yes, I suppose, but for a practicing manager, it illustrates much better the concept of reinforcement—a topic that will be covered in-depth later in this book.

One manager I worked with held onto critical information until we basically begged for it, or we went around him to find out critical things that we needed to effectively perform our jobs. Further diagnoses revealed that his reasoning was more power-related rather than a lack of communication skills. By holding on to critical information, he perceived himself to have more value. The point is this: Most of the time, a diagnosis of communication is like spinning your wheels. Get to the root of the issue if you want to solve the problems.

Much of what gets blamed on communication issues actually is a function of how the human mind works, and how we perceive and process information. Let's first examine how the mind works, and then return to some practical organizational examples.

Perception and the Human Mind

Think of your brain as a personal computer. Your long-term memory is your back-up data that is stored on a CD-ROM somewhere; your short-term memory is your hard drive; and your sensory memory is analogous to your computer's memory (if you don't "save your work," it is lost forever).

The difference between humans and computers is that humans have a more difficult time choosing what to work on. We are constantly bombarded with stimuli, and our sensory memory filters out what it deems not important. As I write this, my wife is asking me why I can't hear our four-year-old screaming in the background. Well, I can now, but, before, my mind was filtering it out (how convenient!).

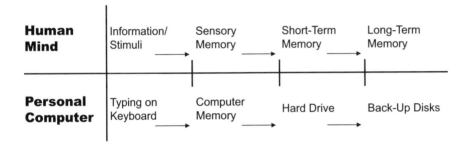

Most of us have had small things happen to us that convince us that our memory is fading, but in reality, our minds just chose not to register the experience on our hard drive. Have you ever been on a trip and have no recollection of driving through a certain town that you know you passed? You may think you were driving dangerously since you don't remember it, but in reality, you most likely just chose not to store the experience. Do you ever get to the end of your shower and can't remember if you shampooed your hair? No, you are not losing your mind; this is the filtering process that the sensory memory uses to determine what to save and what to discard.

In seminars, I ask participants to look around the room and count the number of people wearing a red shirt. Then, I have them close their eyes and ask them to tell me how many participants are wearing blue shirts. While agreed that this is an unfair test, it does show how we filter information. This is why two people come away from a meeting with a different version of what happened, why two people have opposite reactions to being yelled at by the boss, or why one person can think the restaurant service was great, the other horrible.

This is called *perceptual selectivity*. Because we cannot organize and process all that our senses observe, we take bits and pieces. The key is that bits and pieces are not chosen at random but, rather, are based on things such as our own interests, backgrounds, and biases. As an aviation buff, I often hear airplanes flying overhead that others filter out. I can be in a meeting, hear the faint sound of a nice turbine engine, and my eyes turn toward the window; others don't hear a thing.

In the opening story of this chapter, I'm certain that our president could very well have thought that the sales manager was defying him by boldly saying that he wasn't going to attempt to reduce receivables and, in fact, increase receivables as a market penetration strategy. I'm also certain that the sales manager was not doing this; it is just that, for whatever reason, his brain chose not to register that portion of the president's comments.

In many cases, we are processing stimuli that are below our conscious threshold. This is called subliminal perception. Malcolm Gladwell calls this "thin-slicing." He discusses how art experts instantly knew a statue was a fake, but they could not express why. They just "felt" funny about it. Further examination proved that the art experts were correct, but the information processing occurred below their conscious threshold, and they could not articulate why.

Psychology uses optical illusions and little tricks like this sign to give us some insight as to how the human mind works. Most people will filter out the second "the" in the adjacent figure. There is much more to processing and storing information than simply deciding to move it from sensory memory to your hard drive.

Count the number of F's in this passage:

FINISHED FILES ARE THE

RESULT OF YEARS OF SCIENTIFIC

STUDY COMBINED WITH THE

EXPERIENCE OF YEARS

The correct answer is six. If you found fewer than six, your mind was most likely interpreting the word of as a "v" sound.

Here is another one that I received via email:

Aoccdrnig to rscheearch at an Elingsh uinervtisy,

it deosn't mttaer in waht oredr the ltteers in a wrod are,

the olny iprmoetnt tihng is taht frist and lsat ltteer is at

the rghit pclae. The rset can be a toatl mses and you can

sitll raed it wouthit a porbelm. Tihs is bcuseae we do not

raed ervey lteter by itslef but the wrod as a wlohe.

I don't know the research behind this, as the original source is not known. I'm sure the order of letters does matter in certain contexts, but it was an interesting email.

So our minds are very complex, and these activities, illusions, and plays on words illustrate this. Understanding this concept has made me a much better manager. I no longer assume that people are defying me, not listening, not communicating, or lacking motivation. This understanding gives me a wider set of solutions to draw upon to solve problems. By being aware of the biases and limitations of our mind, we can simply make better decisions.

Job Interviews, Performance Evaluations, and "Thin-Slicing"

Statements such as "perception is reality" or "you never get a second chance to make a first impression" are clichés because they are true. Managers act upon perceptions, and job interviews and performance appraisals often feel like first dates.

What is it about a first date that makes us so nervous? Quite simply, we know that one wrong move has such a strong bearing on our future. I'm reminded of one of my favorite lines in the now cancelled NBC-TV show *Ed*. One of the nerdy characters in the show had been trying to get a date with the most popular girl in his high school class. The date went perfectly, until the end when he said, "I had a really good time. I really thought you would be more stuck up than you really are," or words to that effect. You see, I can say this type of thing to my wife and get away with it, but if it occurs on a first date, the relationship is terminated. The "reality" is that they did not date anymore.

Many studies show that job interviewers make decisions about job candidates in less than five minutes. One researcher concluded that up to 85 percent of the interviewers had made up their minds before the interview began based upon the application form and the candidate's personal appearance. How can they do that if they are not using first impressions? The whole thing is scary and yet, at the same time, reality.

This also relates to Gladwell's thin-slicing concepts. We are making decisions based upon small slices of information. He cites one expert who can watch a 15-minute videotape of a husband and wife talking and be able to predict with 90 percent accuracy whether or not that couple will be married 15 years from now. Yes, many factors go into the success of a marriage, but certain factors are better predictors than others.

These perceptual issues play an important role in the interview process. While we all tend to rely on first impressions and thin-slicing, it is important to be aware of the errors that we can make by doing this, with the goal being to improve the process.

For example, we tend to see in others the characteristics that we have, which we automatically assume are good things. This is related to a concept called assumed similarity. We tend to assume that others are "like" us when it comes to what motivates them, what they are thinking, and how they behave.

This becomes something to watch for in the selection process, because I will also assume that my behavior, traits, and attitudes are the best for the organization. In other words, if someone is like me, I will be biased toward hiring that person.

Another perceptual error that we make is that we see one particular characteristic and assume other traits about the candidate because of this. This is called the halo effect. An example of the halo effect would be to assume that if I am a sharp dresser, I must also be well organized, on time, and very detail oriented, when this may or may not be the case. Related to this is the concept of stereotyping, in which we assume things that may or may not be true based upon a group in which I belong.

These particular perceptual biases become even more real when we are under pressure to hire. The work is piling up, we are behind, and we have to get someone hired. We then rush through the interview and end up making a bad decision.

One solution is to focus on designing questions that will minimize your chance of making such errors. Make a list of questions that relate to the job, stick to the questions, and understand the power of the human mind.

I organize and deliver leadership programs. One organization I work with has a month-long program at our campus facility a few times per year. Because the participants are here for a full month, I get to know some of them fairly well. One morning when I was not their instructor, I happened to get a cup of coffee from our break area at the same time the class was on break. I talked to a couple of the participants that I knew, then went back to my office and continued to work. The next time I got up to get a refill, the group was on break once again. One of the participants joked, "You must not do much around here, you are always getting coffee!" To which I responded, "It must be a pretty easy session this morning; every time I've gotten coffee, you've been on break!"

This is classic thin-slicing by both parties. It doesn't matter which party was technically correct, because decisions are made based upon perceptions. My career could hang in the balance based upon incidents like this. What if it were my boss who saw me at the coffee machine multiple times and he was determining who was to get promoted? Let's also assume that all other factors are equal, and it comes down to two candidates. My boss may perceive me as not the best one for the job because, in his perception, "I think he would prefer just to sit around and drink coffee all day."

No, it's not fair, but we all do it. Think back to the last performance appraisal you received. How much of your work did your boss actually see? Did you satisfy 5,000 customers in a given year, but your boss brings up the one customer who called to complain?

The good news is that thin-slicing can go the other way too. I get caught working extremely late at night, and word spreads that I'm a "hard worker." It doesn't matter that I am working at night because I played golf during the day. Perception is reality!

Customer Service: Perception and the "White Knight" Phenomenon

I have conducted customer service projects both with our wholesale distribution business and at the university. It occurred to me after looking at the comments people wrote on their surveys that maybe we were looking too deeply into defining satisfied customers.

What intrigued me the most were the handwritten comments. The pattern that emerged was that the "little things" defined good and bad experiences; and these tended to be centered on the *people* that the customers were interacting with, rather than on the details of the specific problem.

For example, the serious issues that you would think would really upset customers, such as receiving an incorrect bill, someone missing an appointment, or being shipped the wrong product, didn't really bother them. Instead, it was the attitude of the person they worked with when trying to solve the problem.

It seemed as if the most satisfied customers were the ones who were actually getting really poor service. Comments centered on how quickly we fixed mistakes and how cheerful we were when fixing them.

Aren't the easiest mistakes to fix the big ones? We know *how to* fix them, and the customer thinks of us as almost heroic for being able to fix things so quickly; hence, I call this the "White Knight" phenomenon of customer service. Make a huge mistake and look like a hero for fixing it. It is much more difficult to restore customer faith when the problem relates to an employee saying something rude, being put on hold for a long period of time, or not receiving a returned phone call in a timely fashion. The problem is twofold. First, we rarely find out about the problem, and, second, these types of things are hard to fix.

> *NOTICE TO OUR GUESTS:*
> *If there is anything you need and don't see, please let us know, and we will show you how to do without it.*
>
> Mary Toarmina
> McWilliams Fadden

Think back to the last time you had a great experience with an organization, such as a convenience store or a restaurant. What comes to mind? I'm guessing you did not think of a certain convenience store because the quality of their candy and soda is superior. It is probably related to the positive feelings you received while shopping there, perhaps because of the friendly cashier. This concept is called customer engagement and will be detailed in Chapter 7.

My wife and I were dining at a new pizza place. When the pizza arrived, my wife said the pizza was cold and asked for it to be heated more. The waitress actually said that the pizza was not cold because she witnessed it being taken out of the oven. Although the waitress eventually gave in and reheated the pizza, by not understanding perception, she lost potentially valuable customers, because we just don't feel like going back.

You see, the pizza may have been very hot when viewed through the lens of the waitress, but that is not the point. This is what is meant by "the customer is always right." They are not always objectively right, but because they are paying the bills, their issues need to be viewed through their eyes, not through management's eyes.

As is human nature, we don't spread stories around about excellent service, but we do tend to spread the word about bad experiences. I'm sure most people in customer service have experienced the frustration of serving thousands of people flawlessly, but having the boss get on you for the one person who called in upset. This is perception in action and also sort of an informal performance appraisal, isn't it? I've concluded that people can handle major mistakes with organizations, because all organizations make them. What people have a difficult time getting over is being treated in a poor fashion.

Attribution Theory: How What We Believe Affects What We Do Next

The evening that I flunked my first exam as a new MBA student is forever imprinted on my brain. The class was Managerial Economics, and I really thought I had studied for the test. I had read the chapters through at least once and did not miss one single class. I didn't recognize some of the material on the test, but, hey, it's graduate school, it's supposed to be difficult, right?

As I nervously awaited the return of my test, I turned to the guy next to me. He was dressed in a fancy suit, as if he just got off work.

"That was a tough test last week, right?" I asked, trying to confirm that I was not alone in this.

"I didn't think it was too hard," he said.

I caught a glimpse of his score. 92/100, and an A written in red. I thought this guy must not have any hobbies other than studying.

The instructor handed me my test, flipping it upside down so as not to let anyone see my score. A quick glance showed a 42/100, with the letters D/D- written next to it (I guess the professor couldn't decide on a grade).

You need a B to pass the course, and I was well below that. I studied, so that can only mean one thing: I don't have the ability to get a graduate degree. My mind just didn't work like these people's minds. I'm just not cut out for graduate school.

But an MBA would be nice, and I know I'll feel like a failure if I don't make it. I wondered if I could get into another school.

I'm sure we've all had failures in our lives, and how our mind processes these failures really affects what our behavior will be in the future. After failing the exam, there were many directions that my mind went, but all of those directions were designed for me to process *why* something like this could happen. An attribution is an explanation for why things happen to us. If my mind is a computer, consider all of the possible attributions it could have picked from. Here is just a sample:

I didn't study.

I'm not smart.

I got unlucky.

I didn't feel good.

The instructor doesn't like me.

I don't understand the textbook.

My friends kept me up late partying.

I'm not a good test-taker.

Why does it matter which attribution I choose? I flunked the test, didn't I? Well, let's put the attributions in two categories. The first is whether or not the attribution is inside me, or outside me. "Inside me" means things

like my ability or whether I felt good, for example. Outside attributions
are outside the person, such as luck, bad instructor, and the like. Using
that, let's look at the list again, using I for internal and E for external
attributions:

I didn't study.	I
I'm not smart.	I
I got unlucky.	E
I didn't feel good.	I
The instructor doesn't like me.	E
I don't understand the textbook.	I
My friends kept me up late partying.	E
I'm not a good test-taker.	I

The second category is whether or not the attribution can be changed
or not. This is called stable or unstable. Stable means it is not likely to
change in the near future or, for this purpose, before the next exam. If I
think I'm not smart, that is pretty stable, unless I can find some "smart
pills" at the pharmacy. So, using S for stable and U for unstable, consider
the following:

I didn't study.	I U
I'm not smart.	I S
I got unlucky.	E U
I didn't feel good.	I U
The instructor doesn't like me.	E S
I don't understand the textbook.	I S
My friends kept me up late partying.	E U
I'm not a good test-taker.	I S

Some of these are debatable. For example, if you attribute failure to not
feeling well, it makes a difference whether you don't feel good because
of a hangover, because you can change that, or because you have a long-

term illness, for which you have no control. But let's assume the previous frameworks are true for my particular head. If you are the instructor, and your objective is to try to get me to study harder for the second exam, which attributions do you prefer that I have? The answer is anything with an IU. By definition, I'm saying the reason I failed is under my control, and that I can change it.

The worst category for this would be ES. You are attributing the cause to something outside you for which you have no control. The problem is that you as the instructor cannot tell what is going on in my head. You may be pounding on me to study harder, but if I'm saying things like, "I'm not smart," or "The instructor doesn't like me," I probably won't study for the next exam. My mind did not say to me that the cause of the failure was a lack of studying, so why would I even consider studying more for the next exam?

Plug in your own analogies. If your sales force isn't meeting quota, and you think it's because they are not making enough sales calls, they will not make more sales calls if they are saying that the product is overpriced (ES). You will be banging your head against the wall for nothing.

> *Success is simply a matter of luck.*
> *Ask any failure.*
>
> Earl Wilson

After my failed test in my MBA program, I met a student who changed how I studied. We were assigned a group project, and the amount of work he put into this project far exceeded my level of effort. What I realized by interacting with him is that it takes a different level of commitment to succeed in graduate school. Students are not being asked to memorize lists of things, but rather to really understand and apply the material.

Through observing his study habits, I resurrected my academic career, passed the Managerial Economics class (I doubled my score on the second exam!), and went on to receive my MBA. I was only successful because I changed my attribution. After getting that first test back, I was firmly convinced that I was not smart (IS). Meetings with this student showed me that I was not studying hard enough, or in the correct way (IU). This changed everything.

I really like athletic analogies, because they often illustrate how we know these principles, but don't apply them to management. I've had numerous golf outings in which four people are required to play on the same team. This is called a "scramble" format in which four people hit from the same shot and take the best one until the ball is holed. If we have a really good putter on the team, and he misses his first putt, I try to instantly say things to make sure he attributes this failure to an EU event. I may deceive him and say that I saw the ball hit something on the green, or point out that this green is terrible, or say that they put the hole in an unfair spot. Why? Consider the opposite attribution. If he starts thinking he is a terrible putter, or his game is off today, then we have little chance of succeeding.

This also brings up the point about successful events. Let's change the story around a bit and assume that I got an A on the first exam. I will also search for the cause of this, and using the same database from the previous example, should have something like this:

I studied really hard.	I U
I'm brilliant.	I S
I got lucky.	E U
I felt great!	I U
This instructor likes me.	E S
What a great textbook.	I S
My friends let me study.	E U
I'm an awesome test-taker.	I S

We might debate whether or not this changes the classifications, but the point is that when I succeed, and attribute the cause to studying, I'm likely to study for the second exam. A whole new set of issues arises when I'm totally wrong about the attribution. If I really believe I got lucky, I may tend to rely on luck to pull me through the second exam also. Your mind operates like a computer, and what program the computer runs largely determines future behavior.

Learned Helplessness

The stress literature has identified a condition called *learned helplessness*. This is the belief that you have no control over your situation. Learned helplessness occurs when you just accept stressors or bad things without making an attempt to fix the situation or make things better. The academic reason why you can be this way can be explained by the same IU-ES attribution framework.

What if, for example, I told you that I had a friend who has been unemployed for over 10 years? He has now turned to welfare, and things are getting worse. He is able-bodied, but just seems to have "lost it." Typically, our first reaction would be to call this person "lazy" or "unmotivated." This is how the behavior looks, but an explanation can be found if we look into his attribution patterns.

People who suffer from learned helplessness tend to attribute failure to internal, stable events (IS). Therefore, when they get fired from a job, they say things like, "I have no ability, and this will never change," which is an internal stable (IS) response. The learned helplessness aspect comes when things go well. Successes, when they happen, elicit an opposite external, unstable (EU) response. So, they get a good job, they think that they are lucky, and this surely can't last. If they do get fired, the tables turn, and now they perceive this to be a personal failure. The cycle continues until they have convinced themselves that this is just the way things are.

Summary of Key Points

- Although communication problems do exist, diagnosing problems this way hampers an organization's ability to move forward. If you are tempted to diagnose a problem in this fashion, be prepared for lengthy delays in solving the problem.
- Our minds have to filter out items deemed unimportant to us. Because we are bombarded by so many stimuli at once, our brains have no choice but to sort out what to interpret and what to store.
- This brain process helps explain why two people can leave a meeting with different interpretations of what happened, why a worker can be viewed by one manager as a good performer, but be viewed as a poor performer by another manager, or why a waiter can think he is delivering excellent service but, in fact, is not.
- Be particularly careful with job interviews and performance appraisals. These are two management techniques that are particularly susceptible to perceptual errors.
- Even complex topics like customer service often times can be explained by understanding human perception.
- Attribution theory is about how we explain to ourselves the causes of events and is useful in predicting future behavior.

Selected References

For more information on how the human mind works in a management context, see D. Statt, *Using Psychology in Management Training: The Psychological Foundations of Management Skills* (London: Routledge, 2000).

A good resource for understanding the errors humans make during the job interview process can be found in G. Dessler, *Human Resource Management* (Upper Saddle River, NJ: Prentice Hall, 2003). His chapter on interviewing details numerous studies that show the perceptual biases that humans bring to this process.

The concept of thin-slicing is from M. Gladwell, *Blink: The Power of Thinking Without Thinking* (New York: Little, Brown and Company, 2005).

The "Finished Files" activity is from R. Carter, *Mapping the Mind* (Berkeley and Los Angeles: University of California Press, 1998).

Attribution theory has been widely studied in management. Details on the internal-external framework are at H. Kelley, "The Processes of Causal Attribution," *American Psychologist*, Vol. 28 (1973), pp. 107-128.

Another common source on attribution theory is from B. Weiner, "An Attributional Theory of Achievement, Motivation and Emotion," *Psychological Review*, Vol. 92 (1985), pp. 548-573.

For more on learned helplessness, see M. Martinko and W. Gardner, "Learned Helplessness: An Alternative Explanation for Performance Deficits," *Academy of Management Review,* Vol. 7 (1982), pp. 195-204.

2

Personality:
How "Who You Are"
Affects How You Work

"I just don't like sales.
What is the matter with me?"

I t is 5:30 in the morning. The alarm is going off, and I don't really want to get up (who does at 5:30?). I can't stand the days in which I have to fill in for salesmen who are on vacation. Today, it is Doug. He is playing in a golf outing at a really nice country club in a big fundraiser for the local hospital. I should be playing in the outing, not him. Doesn't he know this? OK, it is time to make my way toward the shower. At least I don't have to do this every day. Plus there are 19 customers to visit, and I can't go home until I see them all.

Fast forward a couple of hours. It is now mid-morning, and every single customer has asked me why I'm wearing a tie when it is 95 degrees outside. This is usually followed by them asking, "Where is Doug?" The answer is Doug is at the golf outing, not me, and ties are required all of the time, not just when the weather is nice! Can't they just be quiet while I'm trying to work? OK, I really need to be more social. These are good people, plus, I'm selling quite a few Gatorade deals. This will make Doug happy. It doesn't do anything for me, but I must do the job properly, and that means showing everyone this week's specials.

I didn't stop for lunch, because I still had 12 more accounts to see, and two of them took over an hour. I've just left the last customer, which happens to be 45 minutes away from my apartment. How can Doug do this every day? Does he ever just want to skip this last customer and go *home? I am mentally drained. I should have stopped for lunch, which might have helped. I don't want to talk to anyone; I'm hot. Driving home, I see road construction, and I'm actually envious of the work. They get to work nine to five, they don't have to wear ties, they don't have to get in and out of their cars 19 times a day, and they don't have to tell 19 different people that "Doug is at a golf outing today!"*

The next morning, I settle into my big office chair with a large cup of coffee. I feel like I did so much yesterday that I deserve to take it easy today. I stroll out to the front counter where Bob is in for his weekly visit. Bob is a representative from one of the major candy companies. His job is to take new products directly to the grocery stores, and he gets the products from us, hence the weekly visits. I asked him how he was doing, and he muttered, "Fine, Steve, 5,208 to go." Last week it was 5,216. Yes, this middle-aged man with a good job was actually tracking his days until his retirement!

With another salesman on vacation tomorrow, I knew exactly how Bob felt. In fact, I tried to make him feel better by saying some typical phrases such as, "That is why they call it work, if it were fun, you wouldn't get paid," or it's "hump day," meaning all downhill until Friday, and my favorite, "Thank God it's Friday."

I was becoming another Bob and didn't know it.

Matching Who You Are to What You Do

I kidded myself into thinking that everyone felt this way about work. I asked Doug how he could do what he did day in and day out over the course of many years. He was surprised at how much I could dislike sales. It turns out he could never be in a job in which he was stuck inside a warehouse, managing people, coordinating activities, and throwing boxes around, which is what I liked to do.

The key is matching who you are to the job. Too often, however, we just assume that people can fit in any position, as noted in this story:

JP actually enjoyed working. We all have our moments of satisfaction, but this guy had something wrong with him, because work was just not that fun to normal people. I don't know when he got to work in the morning; I was always there at 6:00 sharp and never beat him in.

His energy was contagious. He was the type of manager who made the whole crew strive to keep up with him. Even though he wasn't the supervisor, he was our informal leader that we followed. Break was over when he got up. If an emergency delivery needed to be made, we did it, because we knew he would be disappointed if we didn't. What a lesson in leadership. Love what you do, and set a good example.

Well, when you are a really good performer in this organization, the logical path to promotion is in sales. He was offered a promotion, and accepted it, mainly because nobody turns down sales—to do so would be the same thing as quitting.

JP looked good in his new role and performed well, but he had clearly lost his fire. In fact, I recall him anxiously waiting to finish up his sales route so that he could "get back to work with us." At the end of the day, he would strip off his tie and go into the warehouse to do what he really loved. After a few months of this, JP decided that he would rather have his old job back.

The problem in this example is that "management" and "sales" are careers that require almost opposite personality types in order to be consistently successful. This is why I cringe when great salespeople are promoted to sales managers. When it doesn't work out, organizations experience what amounts to a double loss: They lose a great salesperson, and they gain a poor manager.

We weren't talking about personality and performance back then, but I'm sure we would have lost JP had he been forced to continue in sales. How many "would-be top-notch performers" are stuck in the wrong jobs? How many Bobs do you have in your organization counting down the days until retirement?

It is really sad if you think about it. We have everything in America. We have wealth, free markets, and the freedom to choose what we want to do for a career. One simply shouldn't go through life in a career that is not a fit. We simply put too much time into work to not have it be meaningful and enjoyable.

The starting point to great management is to first realize how important the fit is between who you are and the job you do. We are all wired differently and have strengths and talents for different things.

Jack Welch, former Chair of General Electric, was a big proponent of removing the bottom 10 percent of his employees at regular intervals. You see, if you are in the bottom 10 percent, it doesn't make you a bad person, but, rather, you're not a good fit for the job. If you can't get out of the bottom 10 percent, who benefits? These people should not necessarily be terminated, because they are most likely a good fit in another part of the organization. The challenge is to really try to understand what the individual's strengths and talents are and to maximize this talent.

I had the opportunity to hear Curt Coffman, formerly of The Gallup Organization, speak about management. He said he went to lunch with some major executives and asked them a simple question: "How long after you hire someone can you tell that you've made a mistake?" The answer: "One week." The follow-up was, "How long does it take the organization to deal with the hiring mistake?" The answer: "Ten years." The organization, the worker, and the worker's family all lose when this happens.

The selection process is a good starting point for fitting people into the right jobs, although a big part of the concept has to do with understanding your own personal strengths and talents. In other words, you don't have to find a new job to harness these principles. It is about understanding how our personality can have such a huge impact on how we view and approach the work setting.

Personality:
More on How the Mind Works

Personality is simply the sum of who you are as a person. Some traits we are born with, while other traits are a function of the environment in which we grow up. Regardless of its source, once our personality is established, it is difficult to change.

Think of the things that you are good at, or the things that you really enjoy. Have you ever had a day at work that just flew by so fast you couldn't remember what happened to the time? How about that meeting, presentation, or project in which you simply performed so well, you couldn't believe it was you?

This happens during the times when you have the opportunity to do what you do best and are making the best use of the paths that have been created in your head. Think of it this way: Our personality is the sum of all of the "pathways" that have been created in our minds. The more we use certain paths, the easier they are to "walk" on and actively use. Some paths were provided for us at birth; others were developed as we grew.

Consider this analogy: Let's say that my mind is trying to get from where this photo was taken down to the beach. There are, of course, many ways to get there. I could just plow ahead, push my way through the trees and weeds, and make my way to the lake.

But isn't there an easier way? A path has been created in the next photo, and it certainly would be easier to use this path. This path may represent the way my mind has worked on previous projects that were successful, or it may represent the types of things I'm good at because I've practiced and practiced. Regardless, it will be easier to get to the lake cognitively if I look for the paths that already exist.

With continuous use, the grass gets matted down, eventually becomes wider, and finally gets paved with concrete as the last photo shows, where the path is so wide that I can ride my motorcycle effortlessly to the lake. The widest paths in our minds represent our talents and strengths. These talents and strengths need to be used and maintained if they are going to be of any value to us; otherwise, they will go away.

For example, I was a good trumpet player in the sixth grade. I was the "first chair" for a number of weeks and did a short solo performance in front of an auditorium filled with parents and friends. Since I only played for two years, my assumption is that a path existed for this talent, and my music instructor developed the path even further.

I lost interest in junior high and moved on to other things. I recently found my trumpet in the basement. I pulled it out of the case and found I was quite rusty after 30 years. I could barely get the thing to make a noise. Trying made me dizzy and out of breath.

What happened? The paths that don't get used eventually grow weeds, and over long periods of time huge trees may grow to make the path unusable. I let my "trumpet-playing path" go into a state of disrepair, and it is no longer usable. Could I repair it? Well, yes, I suppose, but these paths in our minds are basically set by the time we are 15 years old, so it would be difficult to do. This is why it is so important to expose kids to many different activities, so that they can develop their own paths. The more you expose them to, the more paths they will create, nurture, and develop.

It is easier to create these paths at an early age because the mind is still "under construction." Consider learning a new language. I'm sure it takes many years of coursework and practice for an adult to become fluent in a new language. But, my three-year-old son is quite fluent in English. He did not take an accelerated course, and I'm convinced that for at least the first six months, he was not trying to learn language at all!

The point is that he basically learned a language in about 30 months, starting from scratch. Imagine how long it would take typical adults to learn a foreign language if they were just dropped into a foreign culture with no instruction manual. I'm sure it would be a frustrating experience.

My nine-year-old son is learning how to play golf. We were on the putting green practicing short putts of about 10 feet in length. His first attempt flew by the hole, running at least 40 feet beyond the cup and off the green. He looks at me, laughed about it, and ran to get the ball and try again. His next attempt went about 6 inches, prompting a little bit more laughter. After about 10 minutes of trying, he understood the concept of how hard to hit the ball. A path did not exist in his head at all, but as a child, he was good at creating a usable path in a short amount of time.

You need to understand which paths exist for you now. You have a much better opportunity of succeeding and being happy if you design your work to fit who you are, as opposed to trying to make new paths later in life. Yes, you can change, but isn't it easier to work with what you have? In fact, isn't burnout simply the continuous pounding of paths that don't really exist? The following section details how to actually apply this concept.

The Gallup System of Managing to Your Strengths

> *People don't change that much. Don't waste time trying to put in what was left out. Try to draw out what was left in. That is hard enough.*
>
> Marcus Buckingham and Curt Coffman

I have worked closely with The Gallup Organization over the past several years, and their system for helping people identify their own individual strengths and talents is one of the most practical systems on the market today. Most systems focus on personality alone, which is limiting because we tend to just become "aware" of who we are without a usable prescription for improvement. The details of this approach and the Clifton Strengthsfinder™ assessment are included in the book, *Now, Discover Your Strengths*, which I highly recommend.

Recall from Chapter 1 that we are constantly filtering information, interpreting what is going on around us, and responding in our own ways. The Gallup approach shows us *how* we are different, by showing us what our strengths are. Strengths in the Gallup context refer to our most established, widest paths. Some naturally think strategically, with visions of the future in mind, while others evaluate decisions based upon what worked in the past. Knowing where our minds go first makes us much more effective.

What I like the most about the Gallup philosophy is that it is based upon decades of research in which they studied the thought processes and the patterns of the most successful managers. They then packaged this in a highly usable, practical format.

Gallup's strengths-based philosophy is one in which an organization recognizes that the best opportunity to improve is to build upon these strengths and talents, as opposed to trying to "fix" weaknesses. Why try to forge new paths if we have perfectly good paths that are not being fully used?

Take something that you do routinely every day and change the mechanical way that you do it. For example, if you're right-handed, try writing your name with your left hand instead of your right. How did that turn out? Or try shooting a basketball or swinging a golf club with the opposite hand. I truly understand how beginners hate golf after I tried hitting left-handed once! There is simply no path in my head for writing or golfing left-handed.

But many organizations engage in things like "gap analysis" in which they identify what is wrong with an organization. If the task were to improve writing or improve golf scores, a gap analysis would show that we should go to a left-handed writing clinic, or really get out there and practice left-handed.

A bit farfetched? Well, how many of you are told at performance appraisal time what you need to "fix"? This is analogous to your supervisors telling you that you need some new paths in your head. Gallup takes the opposite approach: Focus on your strengths and manage around your weaknesses. This is probably the best thing you can do for yourself personally, and for your organization.

Other Personality Traits

There are many different personality traits and hundreds of assessment tools on the market designed to measure these traits. I want to detail several that have special relevance for people in organizations.

Myers-Briggs

This assessment tool measures how we feel or act in certain situations. The responses are categorized into four broad categories. The first category is about where we draw our energy. Introverts (I) draw energy from their internal world of ideas, while extroverts draw energy from people, activities, and things. The second category is how we perceive things. Sensing (S) is where we take in information through the five senses and notice what is actual, as opposed to intuition (I) in which we tend to take in information through a "sixth sense." The third category is how we decide things. Thinking (T) people have a preference for organizing and structuring information in a logical, objective way, as opposed to feeling (F), which is a preference for organizing and deciding in a personal, values-oriented way. The final category is how we like to live. Judging (J) people prefer a planned and organized life, and perceivers (P) like to be more spontaneous and flexible.

Your scores are then put into one of 16 categories. For example, I am an ISTJ. This means I draw energy from the inside and prefer work settings in which I can decide logically what needs to be done and move toward a goal. I tend to like things structured and organized.

At first, I was troubled to find out I was a very strong introvert. I enjoy teaching and speaking in front of groups and consider myself a fun person to be around as opposed to the nerdy, quiet stereotype associated with introverts.

A deeper understanding of the definition helped me understand myself. I was most unproductive in my career when I was in a position of constantly meeting new people and "networking" in a sales environment. I can do it, and I can do it well, but it requires so much mental energy on my part that burnout would have been inevitable if I had to do this every single day. That path just does not exist for me. My whole profile is more suited for management.

Understanding this totally changed how I approached work. There are fewer thoughts like "TGIF," or "They call it work, that is why you get paid." Burnout occurs when we are in a job that does not match who we are. We rarely get burned out doing our favorite activity now, do we?

The Big Five

At one time, there were about 18,000 words that could be used to describe personality traits. Researchers attempted to distill all of these words into a more usable framework, and the result is called The Big Five personality traits.

1. **Agreeableness.** Cooperative, warm, caring, good-natured, courteous, and trusting.
2. **Conscientiousness.** Dependable, hardworking, organized, self-disciplined, persistent, responsible.
3. **Extroversion.** Sociable, outgoing, talkative, assertive.
4. **Emotional Stability.** Calm, secure, happy, unworried.
5. **Openness to Experience.** Curious, intellectual, creative, cultured, artistically sensitive, flexible, imaginative.

These five have generally been agreed upon as good predictors of performance in the workplace. The strongest correlation to work performance is with conscientiousness. People who score higher on this dimension are higher performing than their counterparts across a wide cross section of jobs.

It is also important to note that not all jobs benefit from high Big Five scores. There is not an ideal personality to have for all jobs. For example, there is evidence that agreeableness and extroversion correlate well to customer service jobs, but other jobs, such as a prison guard, judge, or police officer, actually would benefit from lower levels of agreeableness. You would not want a prison guard or a judge to be totally trusting, would you?

Most researchers agree that these five traits are relatively stable. Therefore, as Gallup research supports, it is much easier to find a job or a task that fits who you are, as opposed to trying to change who you are to fit a certain job.

Emotional Intelligence

Emotional intelligence (EI) was popularized by Daniel Goleman. He defines EI as the ability to both identify and manage one's own emotions and the emotions of others. Are you able to look at someone and tell whether or not they are upset? Do you often lose your temper without warning or are you able to manage yourself?

Goleman found that those who had the ability to delay gratification were more successful later in life. The research methods were interesting. Researchers placed candy in front of young children and told them if they could hold off eating the candy for a short period of time, they could have even more candy. They tracked these subjects over a 25-year period and found that people who could wait actually did better in life. Those who could not wait were more likely to be in jail, or more likely to be pregnant, presumably due to low levels of impulse control.

Goleman's work was originally focused on the educational community. In fact, he was a proponent of teaching the principles of emotional intelligence in grade school. Remember, this is when our pathways are still under construction; hence, teaching young students how to read and manage emotions will be easier at younger ages.

For managers, this is tremendously useful. One study was conducted with scientists and engineers at AT&T's Bell Labs. About 15 percent of the scientists were judged to be star performers as compared to everyone else. The reason they were judged as stars had more to do with their EI dimensions, as opposed to academic performance or IQ. It is most often the social skills that separate the good performers from the stars.

The good news is that we tend to naturally get better at the EI dimensions as we get older. It is not a fixed personality trait that we are "stuck with" after age 15.

Internal or External Locus of Control

This trait measures the level of control that we think we have over things that happen to us, good or bad. High "internals" view the world through the lens that they are in control. When they make a sale, win an athletic contest, or get fired from a job, they attribute the reason for this to factors internal to them. They say things to themselves like, "I am a good athlete, that is why I won," or "I am a lazy worker, that is why I got fired."

High "externals," when confronted with the same events, think that outside forces are at work, and that they cannot control them. They still can succeed, but they may attribute the reason for success to things such as luck or chance, or, in the case of getting fired from a job, they may blame the economy or a bad boss.

We all come up with reasons for why things happen, and as a manager, you need to recognize how "internals" versus "externals" will respond to your management. For example, a high internal will respond well to your suggestion to increase sales by making more cold calls; whereas, a high external might ignore this suggestion, thinking that the reason sales are down is because the price of the products is too high. This is related to attribution theory discussed in Chapter 1, but this stream of research shows that humans may be predisposed to respond with a certain category of attribution.

We do have research showing that high externals are less satisfied with their jobs, are absent more, and are less involved in their jobs than high internals. This makes sense if viewed through the lens of the high external. Why would you get involved and engaged in a job in which you felt the outcomes were random? Aren't you going to be sick more often if you believe being healthy is just random? Go ahead, smoke, drink, and don't exercise; after all, it is totally random when we die anyway!

The good news, like with the Big Five, is that there is room in organizations for all types. High externals would succeed in jobs that require high amounts of structure, jobs in which they do need to follow "orders," per se. One would also presume that jobs in which there is a high failure rate would be somewhat unmotivating to high internals. Failing to find a cure for a disease year after year would be hard if an internal was consistently blaming herself for the failure.

Self-Esteem and Self-Efficacy

Self-esteem is our global image of ourselves, or the degree to which we like or dislike our own selves. We do have research that shows that workers who have high levels of self-esteem believe that they have the ability to succeed at work, and also have higher levels of job satisfaction. Also, those low in self-esteem tend to be influenced by outside forces more than their counterparts with high self-esteem.

Self-esteem is often confused with the related concept of self-efficacy. Yes, a global image is important, but in my view, it sometimes gets too much attention.

Self-efficacy is simply a task-specific measure of confidence. Those with high levels of efficacy on a particular task really believe they have the resources, the motivation, and the ability to succeed at a given task. It is not the actual skills that we have, but our belief about what we can do with the skills that we have that is especially relevant to human behavior. We have to believe and have confidence in our skills in order to maximize performance.

There is a strong relationship between self-efficacy and performance across a variety of different tasks. Research shows that the higher the self-efficacy, the more likely we will take on the task. In other words, challenges are welcomed when we have confidence. Also, when we are confident in what we are doing, we will put forth more effort to successfully complete the task, and we will persist when faced with problems or failures.

Managers are beginning to understand the power of this concept. We have known about the confidence-performance connection for years. Just consider most athletic ventures. What happens when the free-throw shooter or field-goal kicker *has* to make the shot or the kick in order to win the game? Often, the other team will call a time-out. They call this "icing the kicker," in football. They want him to think about the task that lies ahead, get nervous, replay in his head the kicks he missed, which all fall under the category of trying to reduce a person's level of confidence, or efficacy.

On the other hand, what are the teammates saying to the kicker during the time-out? Most likely, they are saying confidence-building things like, "You can do it," or "You are the best kicker in the league!" They may remind him of how many times he has made the winning kick in the past, but all of this is for purposes of increasing confidence, understanding that success is much more likely with higher levels of confidence.

What is not occurring are attempts to build self-esteem. They are not saying such things as, "Even if you miss the field goal, you are still a great guy!" Why? Because they understand that a global self-image is of little use in performing specific tasks.

This is where I think the concept of self-esteem loses some of its value. I recall a push in grade schools a while back to focus on increasing levels of self-esteem, with the thought being that academic performance would follow. It may work to some degree, but only if your confidence in academic performance goes up too. I recall one editorial that discussed how the United States was slipping in certain categories, but at least the students "feel good about themselves." We should be focusing on task-specific measures, not global measures, if our goal is to impact performance in organizations.

Self-efficacy comes from four different sources:

1. **Mastering a Task:** When we accomplish something, it oftentimes becomes easier the next time. That is why we want experienced kickers kicking the winning field goal. They have higher levels of confidence because they have experienced similar situations.

2. **Modeling Others:** We learn from watching others, and if we watch others succeed, our confidence goes up because we see how they do things and accomplish a task. This is one reason why mentoring programs are effective. By modeling someone who has achieved similar goals, we can avoid the mistakes that

they made; thus, mentoring programs can serve as a shortcut to achieve goals.

3. **Verbal Persuasion:** One of the benefits of positive feedback and sincerely patting people on the back is that it increases efficacy levels. This is especially important when people begin to doubt their ability to accomplish a specific task. It is powerful, but also must be sincere. If I have never flown an airplane verbally persuading me that I can land an aircraft all by myself will be of little help. I can also try to boost the confidence of my students at exam time, but if they don't study, they will not succeed.

4. **Assessment of Our States:** We often rely on how we feel, both emotionally and physically, to create efficacy levels. Anyone who exercises knows that whether you have a good or a bad workout often depends on your attitude and assessment of yourself prior to the workout.

There are many different areas in the workplace in which the power of self-efficacy can be harnessed. One area is training. We often train people so that they have new skills to use at work, but underestimate the power of enhancing their confidence in applying these new skills. Training can be improved by understanding the sources of efficacy and incorporating those sources into programs.

For example, trainees should be given hands-on practice in order to really master the task. They should have models that show them how the task is to be done. These models should be similar in skills to the trainees. In other words, I can't even come close to hitting a golf ball as far as Tiger Woods can, so he would not be a good model for me. Accurate verbal persuasion and feedback is powerful, so you should provide both positive comments and be aware of the impact of negative comments. Also, recognize that trainees will often be under high stress when learning a task and be tempted to "give up." It helps if the trainer points out that this type of stress is a normal part of the learning process and not a deficiency of skills on the part of the trainee.

Remember that the confidence-performance linkage is real, so anything you can do to enhance levels of confidence will really benefit the organization.

The Self-Fulfilling Prophecy

Our expectations often dramatically influence the behavior of others. In one study, Israeli Defense Forces were taking a 15-week training course with four different instructors. The instructors were told that one-third of the trainees had high potential, one-third had normal potential, and the potential of the remaining third was unknown. The truth is that the trainees were all assigned to these categories at random.

Those trainees whose instructors were told had high potential scored significantly higher on objective achievement tests, had better attitudes, and held their leaders in higher regard then the other groups. They did better because they were expected to do better! We treat people differently based upon how we view them.

My cousin played high school basketball many years ago, and I recall one game in which the official was highly respected by both teams. It seemed he had refereed college ball at one time and just had better credentials than the typical high school basketball official. My cousin got whistled for a foul that looked questionable, but there was little protest on my cousin's part, nor from the normally vocal fans. After the game, I asked him about the call. He simply said, "I didn't think I touched the guy, but I must have, because that ref is pretty good."

You see, we actually treat people differently based upon the lens through which we view them. I was working on a project with a person I did not view as competent. I kept following up with him, doing his work for him, and asking him questions, which he perceived as simple. He could tell that I had little faith in his work and would therefore come to my office and ask what I perceived to be simple questions. This, of course, reinforced my belief that he was not up to the task, so I would watch him even closer. Can you see how this cycle can oftentimes never end?

It works the other way too. Treat your team like they can succeed, and they will!

Applying Personality to the Workplace

> *There can be no happiness if the things we believe in are different from the things we do.*
>
> Freya Madeline Stark

While I am a firm believer in the concept of matching people's personalities to their jobs, a word of caution is in order. This is just one part of management, and you need to be careful not to give too much weight to this concept. These traits are all just predictors of future performance, but there are many other factors to consider. A person should not be discounted for a job based upon one personality assessment. Scoring low on the Big Five scale does not mean that a person is destined to be poor at customer service jobs. Likewise, knowing your strengths and talents does not mean you can totally ignore your weaknesses. I am an introvert on the Myers-Briggs scale, but this does not mean I should avoid social occasions or be discounted from jobs that involve working with people.

Application of this material is about how people approach their work environment, as opposed to disqualifying someone from a specific job or career. As an introvert, I get my energy from the inside. Knowing this, I try to do my difficult tasks early in the morning. Tasks like writing this book are much easier for me when nobody is around. Extroverts, on the other hand, probably get revved up to write when they are around other people. Just knowing who you are can dramatically improve work performance.

There are assessment tools available for most of the traits described in this chapter, but I generally do not recommend using them in the selection process. For most organizations, it is simply too difficult to really know which traits would predict success. Too many errors will be made unless you have a very well-trained HR department that understands survey validity, job analysis, and statistics. The purpose is not to create a selection system, but rather to better understand yourself and how this impacts work.

Summary of Key Points

- For maximum performance and satisfaction, people must find a fit between who they are and what they do.
- Numerous paths exist and are created in our heads, and the most efficient and satisfying way to live involves understanding and using these paths.
- Burnout is caused by trying to constantly go down paths that don't exist.
- The Myers-Briggs framework categorizes people into one of 16 categories. It is a time-tested framework but can be difficult to actually put into practice.
- The Big Five framework distilled many different personality traits into five usable categories that are good predictors of organizational performance.
- Emotional Intelligence is the degree to which we can recognize both our own feelings and others' feelings and have the capacity to manage these feelings.
- Internal and external control expands upon attribution theory in explaining a person's predisposition to respond in a certain way to events.
- Self-efficacy strongly correlates to success on specific tasks, and there are specific ways that managers can improve team efficacy levels.
- The self-fulfilling prophecy, while not a personality trait per se, does explain to a large degree, why people do what they do at work.

Selected References

Jack Welch's concept of eliminating the bottom 10 percent of workers is detailed in his book, *Jack: Straight from the Gut* (New York: Warner Business Books, 2001).

The quote on page 32 is from M. Buckingham and C. Coffman, *First, Break All the Rules* (New York: Simon & Schuster, 1999), p. 57.

A detailed description of The Gallup Organization's strengths management, and the Clifton Strengthsfinder instrument can be found at M. Buckingham and D. Clifton, *Now, Discover Your Strengths* (New York: The Free Press, 2002).

Details on the concept and application of the Myers-Briggs tool are at I. Briggs Myers, *Introduction to Type: A Guide to Understanding Your Results* on the Myers-Briggs Type Indicator (Mountain View, CA: CPP, Inc., 1998).

Details on The Big Five personality traits are at J. Digman, "Personality Structure: Emergence of the Five-Factor Model," *Annual Review of Psychology*, Vol. 41 (1990), pp. 417-440.

Details on Emotional Intelligence are at D. Goleman, *Working with Emotional Intelligence* (New York: Bantam Books, 1998).

Details on the Bell Lab study are at R. Kelly and J. Caplan, "How Bell Labs Creates Star Performers," *Harvard Business Review*, Vol. 71 (1993), pp. 128-139.

The concept of self-esteem in the workplace is detailed at J. Brockner, *Self-Esteem at Work* (Lexington, MA: Lexington Books, 1988).

Details about the self-fulfilling prophecy can be found at D. Eden and A. Shani, "Pygmalion Goes to Boot Camp: Expectancy, Leadership, and Trainee Performance," *Journal of Applied Psychology*, Vol. 67 (1982), pp. 194-199.

A comprehensive resource on self-efficacy is A. Bandura, *Self-Efficacy: The Exercise of Control* (New York: W.H. Freeman and Company, 1997).

3

The Psychology of Human Motivation

"Aren't most workers just lazy?"

Once I finished college, I transferred to a different branch location in our family wholesale-distribution business. It was going to be hard not to have Dad around, but I was young, eager, and up for the challenge.

The problem is that I just don't understand what makes these people in the branch office do what they do. We never had a team like this when I was working with Dad. There, everyone showed up at 6:00 in the morning; we worked really hard until 10:00, took a 15-minute break, and went back to work to prepare for the afternoon deliveries. We worked until the orders were out and stayed until the last truck was back at the warehouse. Sometimes this was at 5:00, sometimes 7:00 in the evening. It didn't matter what time it was; we promised our customers next-day delivery, and we always did whatever it took to achieve this.

But the employees at this branch location are just different. The first thing I noticed is that they start at 7:00, not 6:00 in the morning, and 7:00 often means 7:20. That is something I want to change. Yesterday, a delivery driver rolled in with four orders remaining on his truck. This is generally caused by businesses not being open at the time we deliver. These four stops were at the end of his route, prompting this conversation.

"Why did you not finish your deliveries today?" I gently asked.

"I ran out of time," the driver replied.

"It is only 4:45!" I not-so gently stated.

"Yes, but by the time I unload my truck, it will be 5:00."

I had no response. How could I respond to logic like this? I'm just not used to it. Well, the first thing I changed was the 7:00 starting time. I pulled all of the drivers together, gave a motivational speech about how important next-day delivery was, and announced that all drivers would report to work at 6:00 instead of 7:00.

About half of the drivers reported at about 6:15, the others at the usual 7:20. Why are they defying me? Nobody did this to Dad! He told people what to do, and they did it. What am I doing wrong?

Fast forward three weeks. I have most of the team coming in at least somewhere closer to 6:00 than 7:00, but I still have two holdouts. I finally tell them that if they are not going to do what I say, then I would rather not have them on the team. I fully expect this move to shake them up into realizing that I'M THE MANAGER, but the truth is, I have not seen either of them since that day.

The problems I faced at this point in my management career were numerous. First, I did not understand how hard it was to transform a culture, nor did I fully appreciate the work that it took to develop a culture and sustain it. It did not just "happen," nor could it be "changed" by simple procedure or rule changes.

My initial reaction was that it was my job as a manager to keep the team motivated. Dad kept us motivated, so I'll just do the same thing!

Defining Motivation

There is not one singular definition of human motivation. In fact, when I tell people I speak on human motivation, I immediately clarify that I'm not a "motivational speaker" in the sense that I'm going to pump you up and prepare you to take on the world, but rather I speak on "what makes people do what they do."

In fact, the premise that motivation is used in so many contexts precludes us from having one definition. One article classified and reported 140 different definitions of work motivation. But, for purposes of understanding what makes people do what they do, I like the following:

"Work motivation is a set of energetic forces that originate both within as well as beyond an individual's being, to initiate work-related behavior, and to determine its form, direction, intensity, and duration."

Understanding what makes people do what they do is an essential management concept. One fundamental flaw that many managers make is that they assume that what motivates them motivates others too. If I love my job and am at work by 6:00 every morning, then I will tend to assume that those who are not like me are

> *I like work; it fascinates me; I can sit and look at it for hours.*
>
> Jerome K. Jerome

lazy, unmotivated, or at least "different." We rarely pause to explore why I might love my job while others would not; hence, the first words of "work motivation" in the definition are very relevant; we are not talking about motivation in general.

The truth is that motivation comes from the situations in which we are put. We are not born with a personality trait known as motivation. We are all created to be hard-working, productive human beings. It's just that some of us work hard on our families, or on church committees, or on restoring old cars, or on improving our golf skills.

Each individual is motivated by different needs, and the academic frameworks that organize these needs tend to revolve around various categories including the need for money, the need to fit into a group, the need to be challenged on the job, and the need to learn and grow.

The problem is this: Most managers don't take the time to really try to find out these needs. They package people into boxes based upon their own needs and wonder why the organization does not respond the way they expect.

This section will first detail some key theories that psychologists have used to categorize the different needs that individuals have.

The Categories of Human Needs

Here's how a need triggers discomfort, which drives us to do something that satisfies a particular need.

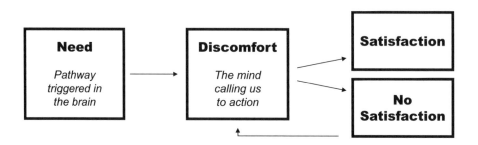

A "need" is simply a deficiency in our body. Psychologists have distinguished between primary needs and secondary needs. Primary needs are generally physiological and unlearned, such as the need for oxygen, water, or food.

Secondary needs are psychologically-based and learned. There are many different secondary needs, but the most common ones are these:

The Need for Achievement

There has been a tremendous amount of research on the need for achievement. Years ago, David McClelland created the Thematic Apperception Test (TAT). Subjects were shown photographs of various events, such as a farmer plowing a field as the sun was setting on the horizon. The subjects were then told to tell a story about what they saw. The high achievers told stories about how the farmer must be sad because the sun is going down and he is nowhere near completion of the task. The low achievers would say the farmer is happy because he finally gets to go home and have dinner. He used this test to propose that achievement is something that can be taught.

Further research by McClelland examined other characteristics of high achievers. He used what is called the ring-toss game to show risk-taking behavior. Subjects were to toss a ring onto a peg, and if they threw the rings from farther away, they got more points. The high achievers chose moderate risk levels—levels that would challenge their abilities just enough. Low achievers, on the other hand, stood very close to the peg so as not to challenge themselves, or they stood really far from the peg where there was little chance for success.

High achievers also prefer tasks in which there is immediate feedback. They would most likely enjoy hobbies such as golf that have instant accurate feedback, as opposed to something like stamp collecting, which is not as high on the feedback scale.

High achievers also enjoy accomplishing a task for the sake of the task itself and are not necessarily doing a task for the external reward. They also become quite preoccupied with tasks once they make a commitment to do something. They are less likely to leave a task half finished.

Consider the typical high-achieving salesperson. They can choose how much time to spend on certain customers and have some control over the pricing. This means that they get to set the "risk level" in regard to making the sale. For example, they can go after an easy sale, hard sale, or one in between. Second, the job has instant feedback with regard to making the sale. Finally, good salespeople get preoccupied with the task and enjoy succeeding beyond the financial implications. The job has the characteristics that high-achievers desire.

What do many organizations do with their very best salespeople? They promote them to sales manager, and oftentimes it doesn't work out. We wonder why the great salesperson has suddenly "lost the passion" when they were so energetic in the field. Well, consider the nature of the typical management position. The primary task involves coordinating people, which does not have instant feedback. The tasks are intangible, so it is more difficult to find things in which to get preoccupied. A salesperson and a sales manager have jobs with different motivational attributes.

The Need for Power

This generally has a negative connotation because of the power scandals that commonly occur in politics and in organizations. We often relate "power and politics" as a negative thing, and rightly so. However, from a motivational standpoint, this is simply having the need to influence people. We could say that controlling people and activities is simply good leadership. Isn't that what management is all about? The need for power is not inherently bad; it's just that power can be used for bad things.

The Need for Affiliation

This is the degree to which we seek approval from others. It can be quite complicated in that the need overlaps with the other dynamics of the organization. For example, sometimes we need to work in groups or have a meeting. It allows the task to get done, but also serves a social need.

I'm fascinated when people make statements such as, "I don't care what others think!" Certainly there is a continuum of people who, on one end, are looking for approval from every person they come into contact with and, on the other end, people who consider themselves independent and not in need of others' approval. But, for a normal human being, it is probably not possible to be totally absent of at least some need for affiliation or approval from others.

The Need for Security

Although we all feel the need to be secure, defining this need is unique for each individual. For some people, security may mean having enough money to retire comfortably; for others, it may mean being assured that they are healthy. Others may feel insecure if they drive a car that they perceive to be unsafe or too small. This also brings up an interesting point about human risk-taking behavior. Look at how some people engage in thrill-seeking hobbies, such as parachuting or race-car driving. Yes, we all want to feel secure, but certainly security means different things to different people.

The theme is that we are all motivated by different things. Let's compare a person who ranks high on the need for security with one who is high on the need for affiliation. They each have been informed of a major promotion and must move to New York City for their new jobs.

What is the first reaction going to be for each individual? The high need for security person will probably wonder if the pay increase will cover the higher cost of living, if the school systems are good and safe for their kids, and if the promotion is really a good thing, regarding the long-term future with the organization.

The high need for affiliation person probably will think about how they will miss their coworkers, how they need to move to a new neighborhood and meet new people, and how they will miss friends and family.

Because our tendency is to assume that others are like us, let's say the manager that informed them of the promotion is a high-achiever individual. The manager is probably going to think that questions about New York City are an odd reaction, as a promotion like this should be nothing but good news.

The Classic Theories: Needs Applied to Organizations

Understanding that we are all motivated by different categories of needs, psychologists over the years have presented numerous frameworks in an attempt to categorize what the human needs are.

The purpose of these theories, when applied to organizations, is to show what motivates us when we show up for work, making the overall point that we are motivated by different things. This is further complicated by many factors, the first of which is that these things change on a daily basis. You may be trying to mend a relationship at work (affiliation need), while I may be worried about my family's safety (I need a bigger vehicle for the safety of my family and am saving up for it).

Maslow's Hierarchy

Abraham Maslow developed what is arguably the most well-known motivational theory, both because it has been around since the 1940s, and because it is discussed in so many different contexts. He did not design it with organizations in mind; we just use it for those purposes in the field of management.

His hierarchy basically states that there are five categories of human needs, and a large amount of human behavior can be explained through those needs. Let's begin by defining the basic categories of needs:

1. **Physiological needs.** Hunger, thirst, shelter, and other survival needs
2. **Safety needs.** Security, stability, and protection from physical or emotional harm
3. **Belongingness needs.** Social interaction, affection, companionship, and friendship
4. **Esteem needs.** Self-respect, autonomy, achievement, status, recognition, and attention
5. **Self-actualization needs.** Growth, self-fulfillment, and achieving one's potential

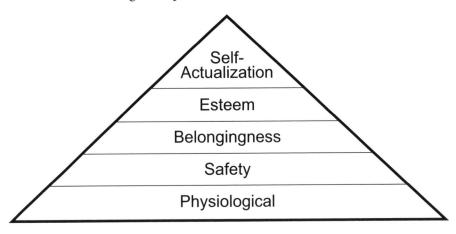

The hierarchy shows that we must first satisfy the needs on the lower end of the hierarchy before we can move up to the higher end. In other words, if we have a physiological need for food, we really won't care about anything else until we satisfy that need. When satisfied, we move up the hierarchy.

While this sometimes works, Maslow's original intent was to show that as lower-level needs are satisfied, the higher-level needs are more likely to become stronger. He was not meaning to imply, for example, that if we are hungry, no other need exists. For most normal situations, we have many different needs occurring at the same time. For example, as I write this, I'm a bit hungry, I'm trying to solve an organizational problem that will boost my esteem needs, I'm worried about my car and am wondering if it is time to trade it in (safety need), and I'm a bit lonely, because I'm the only one in the office (belongingness need).

One part of self-actualization is to "be all you can be," and, by definition, we never really satisfy this need. We rarely say, except for maybe on our deathbed, that we have "done it all."

> *People often say that motivation doesn't last. Well, neither does bathing — that's why we recommend it daily.*
>
> Zig Ziglar

After winning numerous NBA basketball titles, Michael Jordan tried baseball. Following this not-so-successful baseball career, he returned to the NBA. I recall when he went to the Washington Wizards, one sportswriter said that he was making a mistake. He felt that there was no better way to leave the game than to win the NBA title by sinking the last shot. Why should he come back after achieving something as great as that? Well, to me, that shows a lack of understanding about what motivates people. I hit a perfect drive on the golf course once. Should I hang up my clubs? No, we are always driven to achieve more in some venue.

Using these categories, what needs can the organization satisfy? There are things that you can do as a manager to satisfy needs at all of the five levels. Below are some examples of what the organization can provide to satisfy the needs of individuals.

1. **Physiological needs**
   Money buys food, clothing, shelter
   Working conditions, air conditioning, drinking fountains
   Comfortable chairs, good computer monitors
2. **Safety needs**
   Money to buy a new, safer car
   Retirement plans
   Health insurance
   Well-lit parking lot

3. Belongingness needs

Money to join a country club

Money to buy a car

Friends at work

Good relationship with boss

Company picnic/parties

Company softball team

Cross functional teams at work

4. Esteem needs

Money to show you are achieving

Pats on the back

Employee of the month award

Satisfaction from achieving

5. Self-actualization needs

Money

Promotions

Opportunities to be all you can be

So, the organization can play a large role in satisfying these needs. Notice that money was included in each category. There is considerable debate in the field of management on the role that money plays in motivating people. The truth is, almost all of us are motivated by money. Yes, clearly things like a good work environment, having challenging work that we enjoy, or feeling like we are making a difference are all important, but not to the degree that they should overshadow the role that money plays. If you listed all of the potential motivators that exist in an organization, most of them could be taken away for a short period of time with little negative impact. However, think about what would happen if you were told that money was going to be taken away. I'd bet that most of us would not show up for work the next day!

We will cover money in more detail, but for now, note that it can satisfy every need on the hierarchy. Don't confuse "needs" with "happiness."

I am not saying that money can buy happiness, nor should it be your primary goal in life. I am simply pointing out how powerful it can be in an organizational setting.

Can money satisfy the top-level needs? It is clear that we can buy food, but can we really buy friends and achievement? Absolutely! Don't we all do this in some form? I play golf at a certain golf course just to fit in with a group of people. It's not a status thing for me, it just happens to be that that is where they play, and I want to fit in. Most of us buy clothing or cars at least in part to fit in or to be a part of a certain group. It is not shallow or vain, it simply shows the power of money and illustrates the complexity of human motivation.

> *Actually, I have no regard for money. Aside from its purchasing power, it's completely useless as far as I'm concerned.*
>
> Alfred Hitchcock

The top two levels on Maslow's Hierarchy are more complex but can still be satisfied at least in part by money. Consider fields such as professional sports, in which your performance is measured by how much you make. Golfers on the PGA tour desire the "money title," not because they want a bigger jet plane, but because it shows that they are the best at what they do for that given year.

The problem is that, based upon the perception chapter, we do tend to assume that what motivates us also motivates others. As your manager, I might be trying to convince you that if you got your sales quota, you could buy that new boat, but all you want is a day off to take your kids to the zoo. Yes, this can get complicated, but by knowing this, think how far ahead you are of the typical manager.

Alderfer's ERG

The hierarchy does a good job of breaking down the categories, but one conceptual problem is an overlap in the categories. Do I want an SUV for safety reasons or for esteem reasons? Do I play golf with my boss because it satisfies a social need, or because he can help me with my career? Doesn't going out to eat satisfy both a basic physiological need, and a social need?

Clayton Alderfer's theory, while similar in concept to Maslow's, basically condensed the pyramid into more usable categories, with the following definitions:

Existence. Basic things we need to survive or exist
Relatedness. Our desire to maintain interpersonal relationships
Growth. Our intrinsic desire for personal development

It closely parallels Maslow, but recognizes that we may have many needs occurring at once. Again, Maslow was not specifically saying that we climb a pyramid of needs, but the pyramid that we commonly see implies this. The Alderfer model introduced the concept of "frustration-regression," which means that if we get frustrated with trying to satisfy a higher need, we may go backward. In other words, my boss yelled at me at work, so I therefore decide to eat an entire carton of ice cream.

Herzberg's Two-Factor Theory

Frederick Herzberg conducted some interesting studies on human motivation. He simply asked workers to think of incidents at work that made them feel particularly good about their jobs and also to think about incidents that made them feel particularly bad about their jobs. He had them write these down on an index card.

An interesting pattern emerged. The "bad" cards were almost always related to something peripheral to the job itself, while the "good" feelings were related more to job content issues.

He categorized these further into what he called hygiene factors and motivators. Examples are these:

HYGIENE FACTORS

Pay. Basic salary or hourly rate
Benefits. Insurance, retirement plans, and other benefits

Working Conditions. Air conditioning, comfortable furniture

Supervisor Style. Easy or difficult to work with

MOTIVATORS

Recognition. Getting credit for good performance

Advancement. The opportunity to move up in the organization

Achievement. The opportunity to accomplish goals

Growth. The chance to be a better person because of work

Responsibility. People depending upon you to do something

Both factors of motivation are important, but they have different impacts on our motivation and our behavior at work. When you think of "hygiene," what comes to mind? Typically, it is things like taking a shower or brushing your teeth, both of which you probably did today. Is it motivating to you right now? Probably not. We do it, and then we move on.

But what if you didn't do it? If you somehow forget to brush your teeth, it probably would have a de-motivating effect on your day. You would be concerned about both how you look and how you smell, and you would not be able to give work your full attention.

The problem with hygiene factors is that not taking care of them can be de-motivating, but taking care of them is simply expected. I expect to work on a good computer in an air conditioned office. I went home de-motivated once when the air conditioning broke, but when it is working, I don't think of it. Take care of the hygiene factors, but understand what really makes people energized and motivated at work are the growth factors.

One thing I do in my seminars to illustrate this is to have the participants imagine that the thermostat in the room was set at about 95 degrees, and my slides were way out of focus and too small for them to read. Not too motivating, is it? In fact, they would probably give me low evaluations and never return to one of my seminars.

But when those things are taken care of, they move out of their minds. No one has ever written on my evaluation form after a seminar that they really liked how I could focus a projector. Nobody has ever complimented me on my thermostat operation skills. But when those things are not taken care of, they dominate our minds and behavior.

I was a participant in a seminar a few years back, and we were going around the room discussing expectations for the day. One man owned a medium-sized business and was attending the seminar to look for new motivational techniques. He stated that he just completed a market study and determined his pay scale was too low, so he had therefore given all workers a raise. He also just upgraded his facility to put in air conditioning and implemented a 401(k) retirement plan. He noticed very little change in the work performance or motivation levels of his team and was attending the seminar to find out why and what to do about it.

Upon reflection, it appears that this group of theories as a whole explains his problem, and also the power of understanding in how to use these concepts. First, all three of his motivational techniques would be classified as hygiene factors. An acid test that I like to ask is this: Does the factor you are using to motivate make your employees want to jump out of bed when the alarm goes off and get to work, or does it make them want to hit the snooze bar and stay in bed?

Things like pay at market levels, retirement plans, or new air conditioning tend to make us want to hit the snooze bar. But if we have the responsibility to unlock the building, the chance to do a presentation that could potentially land a big account, or have the boss really tell us how well we are doing, we will run to the shower in order to get to work sooner.

The second point is that he was attempting to motivate, in part, by satisfying needs that didn't exist. What do entry-level workers think of a retirement plan? Most likely, they see it as some sort of benefit, but not a huge deal.

What he should do is understand that what he did was a good starting point, but now it is time to move on to the types of things that workers really want: The chance to learn, grow, achieve, and have responsibility.

How Our Expectations Determine Our Motivation

On the first night of my MBA course, I tell students that they should study at least 12 hours per week if they expect to receive an A for the course. I remind them that I was once an MBA student and understand workload from that perspective.

I also remind them that I designed the course that they are taking, further enhancing my credibility regarding workload. It always interests me that not everyone takes me at my word. Some study for six hours, some for three, and some not at all. What would cause people to invest time and money toward a master's degree, then not do what the instructor recommends?

A related example might be in sales. Let's say a veteran sales manager tells the team that if they make eight new sales calls next week, they will achieve their quota. If the same human behavior instincts hold true, then some will do it, and some will not.

The explanation is in part due to personal expectancies. People will be motivated to engage in certain behaviors, like studying or cold calls, when they believe that their efforts will lead to the things that they want, like this example:

Effort ⟶ **Performance** ⟶ **Reward** ⟶ **Goals**

Using these two examples, let's plug in the actual events:

Study 12 hours ⟶ "A" Grade ⟶ Get a raise at work ⟶ Purchase a new boat

Eight Cold Calls ⟶ Achieve Quota ⟶ Boss respects my work ⟶ Get promoted

This nice, smooth progression of thoughts in our head does not always work out as planned. There are numerous possibilities for cognitive "breakdowns" at each point. You see, you are not guaranteed the A grade or meeting the quota just by doing step one. In fact, you won't engage in step one if you don't believe the relationship exists. Therefore, the effort-performance relationship is the probability perceived by the individual that exerting a given amount of effort will lead to performance. As a student, you many have heard that my tests are impossible, and no amount of studying will get you an A, so you don't try. As a salesperson, you may believe that the price of the product is too high, and nobody will buy it anyway.

The second opportunity for a breakdown is in the link between performing and getting a reward. The performance-rewards relationship is the degree to which an individual believes that performing at a particular level will lead to the attainment of a desired outcome. You are also not guaranteed a raise at work or getting respect from your boss by performing. This was my issue as a student. I wanted to earn more money but just didn't make a link between good grades and more money. I didn't think my income would change because of classroom performance; therefore, I didn't study much, even though I had the academic ability to perform.

The final opportunity for breakdown is the *rewards-personal goals relationship*. This is the degree to which organizational rewards satisfy an individual's personal goals. Maybe I'm not motivated by money. If that is the case, the very end goal is not rewarding to me, so I'm not inclined to even start the process.

Your job as a manager is to find out what people have in these boxes—and manage it. If you have a salesperson not achieving quota, ask him or her why. I know it sounds simple, but your job under this theory is to find out where the barriers or cognitive breakdowns are occurring. For example, if they say the price is too high, manage that. Find out if they are right, wrong, or misinformed.

If they don't like the reward you have set, change the reward. I tell my students to get the best grades that they can because they will never regret the effort in the future. I've never had a hard-working student who got an A grade say they wished they had gone for the B instead.

Equity Theory of Motivation

The good news was that everyone was now coming to work around 6:00 in the morning, and they didn't come back with undelivered product. The bad news was that I was now short three delivery drivers. Oh, well, two steps forward, one step back, not bad for a couple months of work. I moved two warehouse workers into delivery positions, which put us short of staff in the warehouse. No problem, I thought that we were overstaffed anyway, plus, I could help out by putting in more time in the warehouse.

That plan worked until the next day, when two people called in sick. Hmm, they seemed pretty healthy yesterday. They would not be sick if Dad was in charge! I knew I was doing something wrong, but I really didn't have time to figure it out. Now, I was behind because I was busy filling orders. OK, I would hire some people, but I really didn't have time to conduct job interviews.

Good news! Dad had two experienced warehouse workers who were eager to transfer to this branch. They were trained by Dad and were good, hardworking employees. I didn't even have to tell them what time we started in the morning.

They arrived within the week and hit the ground running. I was starting to really have fun with the job. Finally, someone else who got what I was trying to do! We occasionally met after work, had a beer, and strategized about our next changes. Bob had an idea that involved combining two delivery routes into one, but it would only work if we had a larger truck. Kevin thought we should try to organize the candy products better. He thought this would cut down on the order-picking mistakes.

A couple of weeks passed, and I noticed that Bob was working slower than usual. He had seemed out of it lately. It might have been my imagination, but he seemed to really get down around me, almost like he wanted me to notice he was working slowly. I didn't think I had done anything to upset him. I concluded that he was simply homesick. I was homesick for the first month I worked here; this must have been his problem too. If this continued, I would meet with him and assure him that this was normal.

It only got worse over the course of the next two weeks, so I finally had to do something about this homesickness. I called him into my office. "Bob, I can see you are not happy here. Would you like to transfer back home?"

"Yes, I would. How soon can I get out of here?"

"Whenever you want. Hey, I understand, I was homesick too when I first moved to town."

"Homesick? Whatever….."

He turned to leave. I was very proud of how I handled this. I had diagnosed a problem, given a good, loyal employee a chance to transfer back home, and I didn't respond to his last comment. After all, what kind of manager would I have been if I had not allowed an unhappy worker to at least leave with his dignity? What 20-year-old wants to admit to being homesick?

In my doorway, Bob turned around and said "Before I go, I just want to know one thing: Why are you paying Kevin $4 per hour more than me? We are doing the exact same job!"

"I'm not paying him more. Why would I do that?"

"You don't have to lie to me, Kevin told me that he was making $4 more than we were making when we worked for your dad. I'm really not upset; I just want to know why!"

I was paying them the exact same amount. I opened the pay register just to make sure he knew I was being honest with him, and after that, things returned to normal. It seems that Kevin, over a beer, simply told Bob that he was making more money purely for his own entertainment purposes. I suppose it did entertain him, but Kevin forgot about it and did not tell Bob the truth.

This example illustrates equity theory. Our minds quickly make comparisons regarding how we are being treated, and we act upon them. What occurs in our mind is illustrated here:

$$\frac{\text{You: Outcomes}}{\text{Inputs}} = \frac{\text{Comparative Other: Outcomes}}{\text{Inputs}}$$

"Inputs" are anything we contribute to the job. This could be hours per week, past work experience, a college education, a client list, dollars in sales, or anything else that we bring to the organizational setting as a benefit. Outcomes are what we personally receive, such as pay, benefits, a flexible work schedule, a really fun job, or the opportunity to meet new people.

The key is, we all make comparisons, but how this actually works in our heads varies among individuals. Let's look at what Bob's equation looked like from his perspective. He stated clearly that he thought that he and Kevin were doing the exact same job; hence, the inputs should be the same. For simplicity, let's assume that both Kevin and Bob worked 40 hours per week, and that Bob was making $4 less per hour.

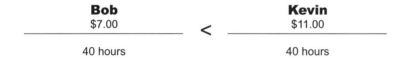

$$\frac{\text{Bob: } \$7.00}{40 \text{ hours}} < \frac{\text{Kevin: } \$11.00}{40 \text{ hours}}$$

Bob no longer has an equal (=) sign but, rather, a less than (<) sign. This leads to bad things, because we are very strongly driven to balance this equation. We have several options available to balance the equation. The first option is to change the numbers. Assuming that I'm not going to give Bob a raise, he still has some options. The first option was one he was engaged in, that of reducing the number of inputs. He would be perfectly happy from an equity standpoint if I cut his hours to 20, even though this brings up a host of other issues.

Equity is also restored if I can cut Kevin's pay or make him work more hours. If you don't think so, look at how satisfied so many of us are when we find out that the very wealthy have to pay more taxes. It doesn't change our situation, yet for many, it seems satisfying.

Finally, Bob has the option of stealing from the organization in order to raise the inputs. Do you know people at work who seem to think it is perfectly OK to steal "a little bit," such as office supplies, postage, long-distance phone calls, or leaving work early? Why else would perfectly honest people feel the need to do such things if it were not to restore equity? This is how powerful an unbalanced equation can be.

As a golf fan, I recall the controversy regarding the Ryder Cup matches when the American golfers decided they should get paid to participate. This prestigious event had always been non-paid, similar to the Olympics. It was seen as an honor to your country to participate. Once word leaked out about the many hundreds of millions of dollars that the PGA tour was making off this event, the players wanted a part of the action. Sportswriters and many golfers alike were taking shots at Tiger Woods and David Duval, saying that as young, wealthy golfers, they did not understand the traditions of the game, nor did they appreciate what events like this had done for golf. They were greedy.

From my perspective, it is simply an illustration of the equity concept. Millions of dollars were being generated by 12 players, and they received zero. Evidence of the equity concept was that Duval stated that they wanted to get paid, but all of the money would go to charity.

Many of you are thinking that if you had Tiger Woods' millions, you would not complain. Try this exercise. Warren Buffett, the world's wealthiest man, has had his net worth estimated at somewhere around $60 billion dollars. For comparison's sake, let's say that when you include your home equity and all of your retirement funds, your net worth comes in at a respectable $1 million. This means that, objectively, $1 to you is equal to $60,000 to Warren Buffett. Continuing the mental exercise, I ask what would happen if Warren Buffett then came to your restaurant, and you tried to charge him $60,000 for an order of fries? Yes, he would be outraged, insulted, and probably would not return to your place of business. Why? Obviously, it is because you were not treating him fairly. This is an extreme example, but hopefully it gets you thinking about the power of equity.

A wealthy businessman in Omaha filed a protest on the tax valuation of his $5-million home. The man is worth millions of dollars, yet he took the time to protest this. I'm sure many people would ask why, but from my perspective, the motivating factor is the same: People want to be treated fairly.

Just Ask Them!

In a recent MBA class, I handed out index cards to the participants. I asked them to write down the one thing that, if it existed in their current job, would really motivate them. The responses ranged from linking pay to performance, getting recognized more for what they do, being able to have a more flexible schedule, or having more freedom to do the job their own way.

I use the exercise to simply show how different we all are, but the point was driven home when I ran across a card that said, "If I could bring my dogs to work, I would be really motivated." I laughed and said, "I guess not everyone took this exercise seriously." Well, to my surprise, a student in the back row said, "That is my card, and I'm totally serious." It seems she is a dog lover and would really be motivated if she were able to go see them on breaks, run with them at lunch, and just be with her dogs during the workday. My negative reaction to her sincere comment was based upon the premise that we assume that what motivates us, motivates others. I'm not an animal person. I don't own any pets, nor will I ever. I, therefore, assumed that her answer was a hoax.

Now, I'm not saying that we should allow people to bring their pets to work. Nor am I implying that if she could have her dogs with her, she would be more productive. But what if you as a manager took the time to really explore what motivated your team? What tremendous insights could you get if you had a pile of index cards that listed the things that would motivate your team? Try it. Sit down with each person individually for 15 minutes and explore ways of meeting their needs. Ask them what would get them to work by 6:00 a.m., what they really need to feel like part of the team, and where they see themselves in five years. You might be surprised at how easy it is to motivate them. What have you got to lose?

Summary of Key Points

- Motivation is determined by the situations we are put in; it is not a trait we are born with.
- Many researchers have categorized the needs of humans. The key is that we are all motivated by different things.
- Maslow's Hierarchy illustrates how organizations can provide things to satisfy many different types and categories of human needs.
- Alderfer's ERG theory condenses Maslow's work and also illustrates how we move from one need to the other (frustration-regression).
- Herzberg's Two-Factor theory shows the difference between hygiene factors and motivators at work.
- Expectancy theory examines the cognitive breakdowns that occur when humans are deciding whether to perform.
- Equity theory shows how humans are driven by the need to be treated fairly and the great lengths we will go to accomplish this.

Selected References

For details on the classic motivational models presented in this chapter, see R. Steers, L. Porter, and G. Bigley, *Motivation and Leadership at Work* (New York: McGraw-Hill, 1996).

The reference to 140 definitions of motivation came from P. Kleinginna and A. Kleinginna, "A Categorized List of Motivation Definitions with a Suggestion for a Consensual Definition," *Motivation and Emotion*, Vol. 5 (1981), pp. 263-292.

The definition offered for motivation was from C. Pinder, *Work Motivation: Theory, Issues, and Applications* (Glenview, IL: Scott, Foresman, 1984).

The categories of needs material was adapted from G. Yukl, *Skills for Managers and Leaders* (Upper Saddle River, NJ: Prentice Hall, 1990).

Details on the concept that achievement can be learned are at D. McClelland, "Achievement Motivation Can Be Developed," *Harvard Business Review*, Vol. 43 (1965), pp. 6-24, 178.

Maslow's original work can be found at A. Maslow, *Motivation and Personality* (New York: Harper & Row, 1954) or A. Maslow, *Toward a Theory of Being* (New York: Van Nostrand Reinhold, 1968).

Herzberg's original theory can be found at F. Herzberg, *Work and the Nature of Man* (Cleveland, OH: World Publishing, 1966).

Alderfer's ERG theory can be found at C. Alderfer, *Existence, Relatedness, and Growth* (New York: Free Press, 1972).

For details on the original concepts behind equity theory, see the book edited by L. Berkowitz and E. Walster, *Advances in Experimental Social Psychology* (New York: Academic Press, Vol. 9, 1976). In this volume, see the chapter by J. Adams and S. Freedman, "Equity Theory Revisited: Comments and Annotated Bibliography," pp 43-90.

Details on expectancy theory can be found at V. Vroom, *Work and Motivation* (New York: John Wiley, 1964).

4

Contemporary Application of Motivational Principles

"Most job are boring, isn't that why we call it work?"

S ometimes the best illustrations of human behavior occur outside of the work setting. Such was the case on one hot July night. I was piddling around in the yard when I saw my cousin Tom arriving, wagon in tow, with two-year-old Brandon inside. They live a short distance from us, and our houses are convenient rest stops when we are out on a walk. Plus, our kids love to play together. On this particular night, my wife and son were at the grocery store, but Tom and Brandon came inside anyway to cool off and have a beverage.

Brandon proceeded to the toys, but, as two-year-olds do, he quickly became bored when playing at someone else's house alone. Tom and I, however, were having a great time. We had a golf outing coming up, and we were trying to decide who should partner with whom.

After about 10 minutes, Brandon climbed on our coffee table. Tom told him to get down. Brandon got down, but was back on the table within three minutes. Tom again told him to get off the table and Brandon again complied. The third time this happened, Tom said to Brandon not quite as gently, "The next time you get on the coffee table, we are going to get back in the wagon and march home!"

Well, it was not even two minutes later that Brandon not only was on the coffee table, but he was doing some sort of jumping-jacks exercise. Tom, visibly upset because he didn't want to leave yet, calmly picked up Brandon, put him in the wagon, and began the short trek home. He then turned to me and said "I just can't get this kid to listen!"

How Humans Learn:
The Laws of Human Behavior

The starting point for analyzing human learning began about 100 years ago with the famous experiments conducted by Ivan Pavlov. Pavlov presented dogs with a form of meat powder and was able to see that a measurable increase in saliva secretion occurred. No learning has occurred at this point because the dogs were born with the ability to salivate.

UNCONDITIONED ————————————————→ **UNCONDITIONED**
STIMULUS   **RESPONSE**

Meat   ————————————————→   Salivation

For the next step in the experiment, he rang a bell in front of the dogs. There was no increase in salivation. But when he paired the ringing of the bell with the presentation of the meat, soon the dogs would salivate upon hearing the bell alone. The dogs had, therefore, been conditioned, or learned to salivate upon hearing the bell. This is called "classical conditioning."

CONDITIONED ————————————————→ **CONDITIONED**
STIMULUS   **RESPONSE**

Bell   ————————————————→   Salivation

The famous "Albert the Baby" experiments involved a psychologist's infant son named Albert. Albert was first presented with various small animals, including a live rat, a rabbit, and a dog. He did not initially fear these animals whatsoever. He was however afraid of a loud gong that his father would ring. Albert's dad began pairing the gong with the presentation of these animals. After only seven pairings, Albert would cry upon being presented the animals, even without the ringing of the gong.

We're told that Albert grew up to be a normal, healthy adult, but I'm sure he feared animals in some form for most of his life. This is the basis for how phobias develop. I have a slightly uncomfortable feeling around grasshoppers. This may sound odd at first glance, but tracing this to its roots makes it clear. I vividly recall seeing a big grasshopper on our front porch when I was four years old. Because it was on the porch, and I wasn't, I saw this at eye level, and it looked enormous.

I'm in a near panic because the grasshopper is blocking my way into the house to find mommy. I scream, the grasshopper jumps, hits my shoulder, and disappears. I then run into the house screaming, telling Mom she will never believe what is outside. But when I return to the porch, there is no sign of this big ugly killer monster. Mom thinks it is my new imaginary friend.

After several days, I was finally able to show Mom what I was afraid of. She simply moved it away with her bare feet, showing me that it is nothing to be afraid of. The event has been burned into my brain, and it takes time and effort to create a different path.

A morning radio show had callers describe their oddest phobias. A sincere caller said that she was terribly frightened of hills, especially when walking. The hosts laughed and thought this was odd, but then the caller said she had twice tumbled down a hill on their farm and had broken her arm both times. This is not a psychological deficiency, but rather simple human learning.

After Pavlov's work, it was recognized that the stimulus-response framework really only explains a small part of human behavior. We don't go around waiting for things to happen to us, then respond. In fact, we operate on our environment in order to get a response; hence the term *operant conditioning*, which basically reverses the framework just described and pictured here:

RESPONSE	STIMULUS
Work $\longrightarrow$	to get paid
Socialize $\longrightarrow$	to meet people
Return to school $\longrightarrow$	to get a better job

Reinforcement Theory: The Basis for Learning

Thorndike's classic law of effect states that behavior that is followed by positive consequences will occur more frequently. Behavior that is followed by negative consequences will result in a decrease in frequency of the behavior.

Or, in other words, people do what they are rewarded to do. People won't do what they are "punished" to do. The fact is, Brandon was jumping on the coffee table precisely because he was getting rewarded to do so because he wanted to go home. In fact, he was listening perfectly, contrary to what Tom thought at the time.

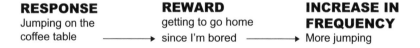

This was a perfect example of what all of us do on a regular basis: rewarding behaviors that we do not want. I do this all the time with my kids. My Sunday afternoons in the wintertime often consisted of channel surfing between the NASCAR race, golf, and college basketball. My kids would make their way right in front of the TV screen. I would tell them to move out of the way, they would giggle, and then move. They would do this again a few minutes later, and I would raise my voice and tell them once again to move. They would giggle, even louder. Now I'm yelling at them to move, and they are laughing out loud while they slide out of the way. Why? The reward was watching daddy "get mad," because they wanted my attention. In an academic sense, I thought I was delivering a punishment, per the equations, when really I was delivering a reward.

Just as common is to "punish" the behaviors that we do want. As a manager of the team of delivery drivers, I wanted the delivery drivers to finish their deliveries as soon as possible so that they could help prepare the warehouse for the night shift. Shelves needed stocking, cleaning needed to be done, and freight needed to be put away.

I noticed that regardless of the weather conditions, or if the drivers had a light or heavy delivery load, they always got back at about 4:30 in the afternoon, shortly before quitting time. It would be easy to attribute this to "unmotivated workers," but a simple examination of the reward structure uncovered the problem. The first people back always got the worst jobs! They were charged with tasks such as stocking the shelves with the heaviest items, cleaning the bathrooms, or putting away truckloads of freight. I was inadvertently punishing the behavior I wanted.

Reflecting on the human learning process, I'm amazed that anyone really grows up normal. When my kids were in their toddler years, I did my best to make sure they didn't play with the cordless telephone. It would get lost, or get turned on, or someone would hit the redial button, and this was quite annoying. I was pretty consistent about not allowing them near the phone, but the confusion came when grandma and grandpa would call. I'm now telling a two-year-old to "come to the phone," when 20 minutes ago this resulted in a timeout!

Types of Rewards: Money, Feedback, and Other Creative Techniques

Money

From a reinforcement perspective, for money to have the most motivating potential, it must be linked to specific behaviors and be viewed as a reward in the eyes of the individual. If every single employee gets a year-end bonus, or a cost-of-living raise, the motivational impact will be minimal.

One organization that I worked with had a year-end bonus system that accounted for a significant portion of the annual pay. Nobody really knew the formula for how the bonus was determined, but clearly it was tied to the overall performance of the organization. This type of system is fine, and certainly has benefits to the operation of the entire system, but from a micro perspective, do you think it changed behavior? It probably did not, because no one can make a link between behaviors and outcomes.

There was a sign on one company's copy machine that said, "Use the copy machine sparingly, bigger bonuses for us all!" The attempt at efficiency is fine, but, really, I think most employees at this company believed they could run the copier 24/7 and not see a noticeable difference in their paychecks. Now, they may be wrong, but perception is reality, and if they don't make a link between behavior and the outcome, the behavior will not change.

Consider the job performance of a cab driver versus a bus driver. Cab drivers are generally considered to be highly motivated, even to the degree that they may drive dangerously. Also, they are very efficient. I've even had two cab drivers get mad at me for taking a cab for a short trip! Why are they so high performing? At least part of the reason can be attributed to the fact that they have a meter that tells them to the penny how much money they are making. How would this change your job? If I could have a meter in front of my desk telling me how I was doing, that would really alter my behavior!

Now, I'm not calling bus drivers low performing; we get the desired behaviors from them, but I've never heard of a bus driver getting mad at someone for taking a short ride.

Positive Feedback

It could very well be that you can't actually pay people for the behaviors you desire in your organization. Things like "teamwork" and "good customer service" are oftentimes difficult to see and measure, so it could be difficult to put a fair reward system in place. The good news is that positive feedback works as well as or better than money—and is free. This is one of the most potent management tools we have and is arguably the most underused.

In general, we assume that workers should know if they are performing well, we are embarrassed by the prospect of patting someone on the back, or we think this type of feedback will "go to their heads." We, therefore, don't even begin to tap the potential of this simple tool. Donald Clifton, the former chair of The Gallup Organization, remarked that he had never run across anyone who had suffered from "over-recognition" in the workplace.

I recall receiving a letter from a manager of a convenience store thanking me for the great service we provided. Prior to this, the manager asked me to switch the delivery from morning to afternoon. I must have passed the message on to the delivery driver, but I really didn't remember doing anything special. But this letter was incredibly motivating to me. Very few people take the time to write things like this. I still have this letter almost 20 years later.

What kind of service do you think this manager received from me in the future? Great service, because I was rewarded for doing it. If I have a list of phone calls to return, she would get the priority, as I was rewarded in the reinforcement sense for calling her. In fact, the concept of "the squeaky wheel gets the grease" actually is not always true. Sometimes, we get new wheels or trade cars.

Contingent Time Off

One of my colleagues conducted a study in which he took a night shift of factory workers that were underperforming. They were producing 160 units per shift with a 10 percent defect rate. The industry standard was 180 with a 5 percent defect rate. He asked the team how their bonus system worked. They stated that they really didn't know, and that the calculations were quite complicated.

So he had them try something new. They were told that if they could produce 200 units with a 1 percent defect rate, they could go home and continue to get paid for the rest of the shift. This was called the Contingent Time Off (CTO) program. Well, they ended up finishing several hours before the shift was over on a consistent basis, with production and quality significantly improved. So basically they went from 160 to 200 units per shift, increased quality and output dramatically, and did this without increasing payroll costs at all.

The bad news is that when the experiment was over, management raised the standard and made them work the entire shift. It seemed as if this proved to them that this group was underperforming. By doing this, the performance level dropped well below what it was prior to the experiment; thus, the CTO program was abandoned. This is just one example of taking a really good management program and making one mistake that sabotages the entire effort. Workers were actually punished for doing good things.

It is easy to think that they were being lazy before, but the truth is they did not have an adequate reason to try to improve their performance before the experiment. I would wager that most of them had no idea what the industry standards even were. When the new program was implemented, they probably got together to strategize about how to get done early, helped each other with equipment, and, in general, did things that they otherwise would not have had to do.

Schedules of Reinforcement

You don't have to reinforce every single behavior to make this work. In fact, one of the most powerful reinforcers is a slot machine. It is on what is called a "variable ratio" payout schedule, meaning we engage in the behavior of pulling the handle, without knowing if we are going to get a payoff.

One application that my students did not seem to like at all was the semester that I tried case studies in my principles of management course. I needed a mechanism to make sure the students had read them and were prepared to discuss them during class, but with 70 students across two classes, I did not want to read all of these every single week. I told them I would collect and grade these randomly. This served the purpose of getting them to read the cases and analyze them, without the need for me to read each and every one. It did have a side effect in that students tried to guess when I would pick them up. Some would be disappointed when they did a really good analysis, and it wasn't a week I chose to grade them. They did do them, and this illustrates the point that you don't have to reinforce each and every behavior in order for this to work.

Potential Side Effects of Reinforcement

As with most powerful management techniques, there are pitfalls to avoid, some of which have been discussed.

Rewarding A, While Hoping for B

Steve Kerr has a classic article in management by this title, and many of the classic case studies in management revolve around this concept. His paper examines many of the things that occur in society, explaining them through the use of a faulty reward structure. For example, the best basketball teams are "best" because of "teamwork," yet players are rewarded based upon individual stats.

At work, we want open and honest communication, but often lash out at those who bring us problems. In fact, one of my favorite case studies involves a small business owner who, in frustration, told his staff, "The next person to bring me a problem is going to get fired." Well, the business went bankrupt a short time later because of unforeseen problems that went unattended.

Any child that doesn't want to mow the lawn anymore knows that a great technique is to mow over the flowers. Dad will then determine that we are not responsible enough for the task, or mom won't allow us to touch the mower again.

Linking Rewards to Behaviors

Remember the entire equation. It is not rewards in and of themselves that have a motivational impact but, rather, rewards that are tied to identifiable behaviors. If the reward is not linked to anything, it won't have an impact on motivation. If the "employee of the month" award simply rotates through all employees to be fair, then don't expect a motivational impact. By the same token, if everyone gets the same Christmas bonus, it won't change behaviors.

This was the same motivational problem with the year-end bonus plan. Again, it has its benefits but will not have an impact from a behavioral standpoint.

What Is a Reward for Some Is a Punishment for Others

Sometimes we think we are rewarding when actually we are punishing. I may think that I am providing a positive reinforcer by pointing out in front of the class the student who had the highest test score. While this would certainly be quite rewarding to some, for many people, this would be embarrassing.

It may sound strange, but even something as simple as more time off might be a punishment to a worker who would rather not go home. The good news is that private recognition and money that is tied to performance are considered "universal" reinforcers in that they almost always work. The key is, however, to be aware of individual differences.

The "If Your Life Depended on It" Test

Many times management tries to reward behaviors that the workers could not do if their lives depended on it. Maybe they don't have the equipment, training, or ability to do what we are asking them to do.

I play in a golf league once a week. It is just a nine-hole league, and most players are beginners. One issue that courses have had to deal with is that of slow play. Slow play is similar to a traffic jam. Usually it is caused by too many people trying to get to the same place, or an "accident" happens that slows down everyone. One player spending too much time looking for a golf ball slows down everyone.

To combat this, the course introduced a "pay for performance" system in the form of a free drink if you could complete your round within two hours. This of course had zero effect on the speed of play and actually added to the frustration level of the golfers. Imagine being in a traffic jam with a reward waiting for you at home, when you have no control.

When the Desired Behaviors Are Dangerous

One reason I never implemented an incentive system for the delivery driver team was that I was concerned that my team would turn into a bunch of taxicab drivers. While I valued basic efficiency, I also wanted good safe driving, along with spending quality time with the customers.

These potential side effects do illustrate how powerful the technique can be. The key is proper implementation.

Designing Jobs and Setting Goals: Structuring Tasks for Maximum Performance

The motivation theories discussed in prior chapters propose that behavior originates inside our heads—thoughts lead to actions, and these thoughts originate for various reasons, all related to what our human needs are.

The reinforcement theories, on the other hand, show us that humans simply do what they are rewarded to do. The truth is both perspectives are correct. Humans do think ahead and plan actions, but they also respond and are aware of the consequences of their actions.

This section deals with the nature of the job itself. Aren't some jobs designed in such a way as to be naturally motivating? Aren't other jobs simply boring?

I was in Atlanta for a three-day conference, and thought I would look up Big Mike. He was a good friend in college, and he recently had taken a job as a buyer for a chicken processing plant in a very small town north of Atlanta.

I found the chicken plant, and Big Mike was eager to give me a tour. I liked those old Mr. Rogers episodes where they showed us things like how candy bars are made, and I figured this would be similar. Well, it was, only it is not nearly as entertaining when seeing how live animals are processed. In fact, I now know why Mr. Rogers chose things like candy bars! If you are thinking of becoming a vegetarian, I highly recommend tours of this sort.

The tour began in a room that was about the size of a small conference room. It had a loading dock on one side and a small window on the opposite wall toward the ceiling that led to the rest of the factory. Down the middle was a mechanical conveyer device that reminded me of the mechanism that many dry cleaners use to store clean clothes prior to pick up. There was one man in this room, and he was picking up live chickens off the floor and hanging them by their feet upside down on this mechanism. They then went through the window into the factory for step number two, which I will save for your imagination.

When the room was close to empty, another semi-truck backed up delivering more chickens. The chickens would run down the ramp into this room where the "chicken hanger" would pick them up and hang them, and off they went. Since the room never was totally empty, I had to wonder if some chickens remained in this room for days on end before succumbing to the upside down hanging. Probably not, but an interesting thought nonetheless.

The rest of the tour was quite interesting, but what stuck in my mind was this chicken hanger. By most counts, most of us would consider him "unmotivated." How could he do such a boring job day after day?

The chicken hanger story describes the typical "boring" job. It is, in fact, the most boring job I have ever witnessed. It took few skills, probably did not pay that well, and, to top things off, it was not very easy to do. Most of us would probably consider the chicken hanger to be unmotivated, assuming that this is all that he does, and that he had no aspirations to move up in the organization.

The topic of job design proposes that a big chunk of human motivation could be related to how the job is structured. In other words, people aren't "lazy," they are just sometimes put in jobs or situations that make them appear lazy.

Compare this with a job like that of a surgeon as portrayed on any of the medical shows on TV, such as *Grey's Anatomy* (ABC). The doctors on this show seem incredibly motivated. They work multiple shifts, rarely take breaks, respond to their pagers at home in the middle of the night, and, in general, seem like the type of players we would like to have on our work-teams. You rarely hear them say things like, "I'm still on my coffee break, you do the surgery."

From a motivational standpoint, is the chicken hanger's brain wired that much differently than a surgeon's? Do they really have different needs, desires, and abilities? Or is the nature of the job responsible for these differences?

Job Characteristics Model of Work Motivation

The concept of job design dates back to the early stages of management, when it was observed that people can get quite bored at work, thus prompting researchers to explore various ways to structure specific jobs to enhance worker motivation. The model illustrating job design is called the Job Characteristics Model.

Five Core Dimensions ⟶ **Psychological States** ⟶ **Work Outcomes**

This model identified five different core characteristics that can be used to describe almost any job. These five trigger "states" inside of our head, and these states predict certain outcomes.

The five core dimensions are defined as follows:

Skill variety. The degree to which a job requires a variety of different skills and talents to effectively do the job.

Task identity. The degree to which a job requires completion of a "whole" piece of work; that is, doing a job from beginning to end, as opposed to something like an assembly line in which each person does one very small part.

Task significance. The degree to which the job has a substantial positive impact on the lives of other people.

Autonomy. The degree to which the job provides freedom and discretion in how the task is completed.

Feedback from the job itself. The degree to which carrying out the work activities required by the job provides the individual with direct and clear information about his or her performance.

These five core job dimensions trigger the following states in our heads:

Experienced meaningfulness of the work. The job must be meaningful in your own set of values. If you don't feel as if you are accomplishing something important, the potential for the task to be motivating is likely to be low.

Experienced responsibility for the work. You must believe that you are accountable for the work. If you believe that your performance is more dependent on external factors, then you have no basis for feeling good when a job is done well, nor bad when it is done incorrectly.

Knowledge of results. If you cannot determine performance, then there is no basis for either feeling good or bad about a job.

When these three psychological states are high, then the organization can expect high motivation and satisfaction, high performance, and reduced absenteeism and turnover. This model does work across a variety of jobs and is very usable in the application sense. If you are not getting the performance you desire, you may be falling short in one or more dimensions.

Can a large component of the motivation be traced to the nature of the job that a person is doing? If the chicken hanger were in a job that was as well designed as that of a surgeon, wouldn't he have a dramatically different motivational level? What if a surgeon were in a job that was as poorly structured as that of the chicken hanger? I do recognize that we have to consider other factors like one person was motivated to go to medical school, for example. But are there things that managers can do for the chicken hanger to make his job better? The research shows that we can, with the following guidelines.

Combine tasks. Combining fractionalized tasks into a new work module increases the level of skill variety and task identity. The chicken hanger could not even see over the wall to the next step.

Imagine what would happen if he were responsible for more steps. Look at how many different tasks a surgeon does on a given shift. We rarely see them in a "rut" because things are "too routine" in the ER.

The key is to combine tasks into naturally better units of work, not just to dump more work on them under the guise of combining tasks.

Establish relationships with the customer or end user. Direct contact between workers and customers increases skill variety, autonomy, and feedback. It is very powerful when you can see the outcomes of what you are doing. Instead of going home at night feeling like he just "hung chickens all day," what if he thought of himself as feeding the world?

This is yet another powerful aspect of the surgeon's job. They are working with the end user, not fixing things or creating a product for someone they will never see.

Empowerment. Empowering employees to make decisions formerly reserved for management increases autonomy. It is also a great application of what Herzberg discussed concerning hygiene factors and motivators.

The surgeon also has the power to do the job his or her way. While doctors are bound by medical standards, ethics, and legislation, they certainly make quick decisions without much argument when lives are at stake.

Open feedback channels. The original theory was referring to feedback that is obtained from the job itself. Landing an airplane is a task that has this type of instant feedback. You don't need to wait for the annual performance review to know whether or not you had a good landing. If the job lacks this type of feedback, then it is management's job to supplement it. In addition to objective information, this feedback can also serve as positive reinforcement.

The job design model only works if individuals do, in fact, have a desire to learn and grow on the job. While this is true for most of the population, certain people prefer not to learn and grow on the job. For them, job redesign efforts will be seen as more work, more responsibility, and more tasks to undertake. This represents a small percentage of the workforce, but must be considered.

Job Design and Human Perception

Job design researchers point out that no two workers will evaluate the same job in exactly the same way. The model still exists inside a person's head, just like the other theories of human motivation. Consider the dimension of *task significance*. I'm sure most of us would say that a drug dealer is doing little to benefit society. However, they themselves may think that they are doing good things by providing entertainment, giving people an escape from their day-to-day struggles, or making people "feel good."

The same is true with our chicken hanger. He can either go home and think that he didn't accomplish anything except for hanging up and killing a bunch of chickens, or he can view his job through the lens of doing his small part to feed the world. Clearly, the lens through which he views this will dramatically affect his motivation level.

The Social Information Processing Model (SIP) says that people respond to their jobs according to their perceptions rather than to the objective characteristics of the job. This model asserts that employees adopt attitudes and behaviors in response to social cues provided by day-to-day contacts with others. In other words, coworkers, supervisors, friends, family members, or customers can have a huge influence on how we view our jobs.

This is a good application of perception discussed in Chapter 1. People respond to their perceptions, so perceptions must be managed. If the team thinks the job is boring, it will be boring.

Recall the classic story of Tom Sawyer whitewashing the fence. His mother charged him with the somewhat boring task of painting the fence, which he did not want to do, and it would be considered a boring way to spend a Saturday by most of us. But Tom's strategy was to make the task look fun, thereby recruiting neighbor kids to help. Not only did he succeed at this, but he had these kids paying *him* to let them help. And they really were enjoying the task. Remember, it is not the objective job, but how we perceive it that matters. This can work in the negative too. If workers are complaining about how bad things are, this can spread.

Try yawning in a crowded room and watch how many others yawn right after you. In fact, I would venture to say that many of you yawned after reading the word yawn. Because human behavior can be influenced by environmental factors, managers should pay as much attention to employees' perceptions of their jobs as they do to the objective characteristics of the jobs.

I would occasionally overhear workers state how much more money they could make if they went to work at the beef processing plant that was across the street from our business. Yes, they could make more money, but the work was incredibly difficult, as I found out from my short tour of the chicken plant. As a manager, I could roll my eyes and think that they just don't know what beef processing work is like, but the power of perception, combined with equity theory, meant that I really needed to manage it. I generally would simply point out that the work was incredibly difficult, smelly, and tiring, and if they wanted to give it a try, to go ahead. I think this worked, because very few left to try it.

Setting Effective Goals

The management article clearly stated that goals work, so I wanted to try it. The first stop was the office supply store. The article said to chart performance, and I needed graph paper, new markers, and big file folders for each salesman. The article also said that it was important to meet with each person individually so they would buy in to their goals. No problem, we meet every Friday anyway, and I need to do something different. The regular sales meetings were getting a bit stale.

I set up 30-minute appointments with each salesperson. They were to come prepared with their goals for the coming year, how they were going to achieve them, and how I could help them.

The meetings went very well. They liked the opportunity to look toward the future. In the past, Fridays seemed to be set aside for addressing problems, accounts receivables, and upset customers. It is fun to do something positive for once.

The article also said that challenging goals are better, so I encouraged them to set their sights even higher than what they came in with. Today, we call these "stretch goals."

After the last salesman left, I reflected on the process and was generally satisfied. We had a good day, got out of the normal "meeting mode," and I got a chance to really sit down with everyone individually. Plus, they liked my files, which made it look like I took this seriously. I bundled the files in a big rubber band, put them in the bottom drawer of the file cabinet, and headed home.

Goal setting is a powerful management tool. When properly applied, goals provide direction and focus to items that otherwise would not get our attention. We then put forth more effort, develop wiser strategies, and achieve higher levels of performance.

With proper implementation, it almost always results in increased performance. To implement goals correctly, consider the following four key points:

Specific. Detailed goals are better than vague "do your best" goals. If my goal is to lose weight, I have a much better chance for success if I am more specific. A goal to "lose 15 pounds by Christmas" is much better than "lose as much weight as you can before the holidays."

Difficult. Difficult goals are better than easy goals. This is because easy goals do not direct and focus our attention as well. If my goal is to lose two pounds by Christmas, it will be easy to procrastinate.

Feedback. Goals need regular feedback. This is why we weigh ourselves regularly if our goal is to lose weight. Think how unmotivating it would be to take an exam, and then be told you would not get your results for one year. I'm sure I would lose interest. The other benefit of feedback is that we are reminded of our progress and sometimes prompted to change our strategies.

Acceptance. Individuals must accept the goal as their own. This depends on several factors, such as whether the goal is attractive and has a reward attached to it, whether we believe it is achievable, and how public we have made the goal.

Now, fast forward six months: It was another typical Friday. I have 12 salesmen complaining that we have been out of 50-pound bags of popcorn for over a week now, and the swimming pool concession stands that purchase popcorn are complaining. I try to tell them it is out of my control, but they still keep asking the same questions. Accounts receivables are once again high, and we just put a credit hold on one of our largest accounts. One salesman tells me he needs a new delivery driver or some key customers are going to quit buying from us and go to the competitor. I've got two delivery trucks in the shop; I don't have time to worry about new drivers today.

This is a typical Friday, but it has been compounded by the fact that we are six months into the new goal-setting program and my sales report shows that only one salesman is on track to achieve his goals. The rest have sales increases, but most of that has been due to inflation or price increases. I don't think any of them have contacted the new customers that they said they were going to contact. Oh, well, no time for this, I have a customer on hold who received popcorn instead of the frozen chicken that he ordered (I thought we were out of popcorn).

Goal setting is clearly a waste of time. It reminds me of when I tried quality circles.

> *Success is not who you know, but who wants to know you.*
>
> Arthur Fripp

My experience was a classic example of doing a management program *almost right*, but failing because of one thing. In this case, we did create specific goals that were difficult, and because of the individual meetings, the salesmen did accept the goals that they set. The program failed because I didn't provide regular feedback. I did not revisit the project for the first six months, so it was forgotten. It was not as though they were not working hard; it is just that they were not working hard on the goals, primarily because they had not received good objective feedback as to their progress.

Feedback reminds us of the goal and also allows us time to reflect, strategize, and re-tool. I should have spent just five minutes a week updating the team as to their progress. That probably would have made a remarkable difference in how the goals were viewed and whether or not they would have been achieved. It is not just because of some fluffy motivational concept either. If the focus was more on the goals, maybe they would have been more effective at delegating tasks, asking me for help, or working together on problems.

Side Effects of Goal-Setting Programs

Because the effects can be so powerful, organizations should be aware of some potential side effects of goal-setting programs. First, be careful not to set goals that are so specific that other important aspects of the job are forgotten. If you set a goal to increase sales, remember to include collecting for the sale as a part of the goal. If the goal is increased production, don't forget to include "quality" production. It sounds simple, but it is easy to forget in the implementation.

Next, be careful not to set goals that are too easy. This can lower expectations and cause people to stop performing; after all, they have achieved their goal. Managers need to quickly set new goals in order to avoid this "ceiling on performance."

Goals can also reduce performance on complex tasks. They serve a function of increasing our individual level of arousal, which is good for some tasks and bad for others. If I am lifting weights, I like to be fired up, mad, and full of energy. That same state of mind does not work if I'm trying to take an exam, type a paper, or make a five-foot putt on the golf course.

Consider the atmosphere at a typical college football game. What if you placed a desk on the 50-yard line and tried to do a complex task such as take an exam, with a stadium full of people cheering for you to succeed? Yes, this kind of support would most likely deter performance for most people.

As an avid golfer, I play my best when I'm at a medium level of arousal. If I get too casual, I don't concentrate, but if I get too much into the game, I don't perform as well. I want to win so badly that I try "too hard" and begin to focus on the wrong things, effectively losing concentration.

Summary of Key Points

- Human learning has its roots in classical conditioning.
- Operant conditioning explains how humans "operate" in their environment in order to receive something.
- Behavior that is followed by positive consequences will result in an increase in frequency of behavior, and, likewise, behavior that is followed by negative consequences will result in a decrease in frequency of behavior.
- Positive consequences are things that increase the frequency of behavior, including money, feedback, recognition, or time off.
- There are side effects and potential pitfalls during the application of reinforcement.
- At least part of human motivation can be attributed to the way the job is structured.
- Jobs can often be restructured in order to be more motivating to most people.
- The concept of goal setting does work when implemented properly.

Selected References

For a detailed look at the behavior theories, see the book edited by N. Nicholson, P. Audia, and M. Pillutla, *The Blackwell Encyclopedic Dictionary of Organizational Behavior* (London: Blackwell, 2004). In this volume, see the chapter by F. Luthans, C. Youssef, and B. Luthans, "Behaviorism."

The classic Albert the Baby studies are detailed in J. Watson and R. Rayner, "Conditioned Emotional Reactions," *Journal of Experimental Psychology*, Vol. 3 (1920), pp. 1-14.

For a discussion on side effects and implementation of reinforcement theory, see the book edited by R. Steers, L. Porter, and G. Bigley, *Motivation and Leadership at Work* (New York: McGraw Hill, 1996). See the chapter by J. Komaki, T. Coombs, and S. Schepman, "Motivational Implications of Reinforcement Theory."

The Contingent Time Off study is at D. Lockwood and F. Luthans, "CTO: A Non-Financial Incentive for Improving Productivity," *Management Review*, July (1984), pp. 48-52.

A classic article on how managers reward behaviors they don't want can be found at S. Kerr, "On the Folly of Rewarding A, While Hoping for B," *Academy of Management Journal*, Vol. 18 (1975), pp. 769-783.

Details on the Jobs Characteristics model can be found at J. Hackman and G. Oldham, "Motivation Through the Design of Work: Test of a Theory," *Organizational Behavior & Human Performance*, Vol. 16 (1976), pp. 250-279.

The seminal paper on goal setting is E. Locke, "Toward a Theory of Task Motivation and Incentives," *Organizational Behavior and Human Performance*, May (1968), pp. 157-189.

The Social Information Processing model of job design is detailed at G. Salancik and J. Pfeffer, "A Social Information Processing Approach to

Job Attitudes and Task Design," *Administrative Science Quarterly*, Vol. 23 (1978), pp. 224-253.

5

Get Real
About Conflict Management

"Can't we all just get along?"

everal times a year, we brought in all salespeople and managers from multiple branch locations to headquarters for a meeting, and it resulted in a nice productive day. This sales force was a very tight, cohesive group. There had traditionally been little turnover, and most had known each other for years, so the social aspect of these meetings was also important, and it was a nice getaway.

In addition to being cohesive, this group was also quite competitive. Sales results were published weekly for all of the salespeople to see, which fueled the competitive culture. We were having a beer after the meeting, reflecting on the day, but mostly giving each other a hard time. Gary and Dale were taking friendly jabs at each other. This started when Gary pointed out that he once again beat Dale in the third-quarter sales contest. Dale seemed to take it in stride until Gary made some derogatory comment about Dale's hometown.

I didn't hear what was actually said, but Dale jumped out of the barstool and gave Gary a hard shove. Gary stumbled back, in a bit of shock, but recovered quickly enough to take a swing at Dale. Fortunately, it was only a glancing blow to the chest. Big Bob was watching from a table behind and quickly moved his 350-pound frame in between the two. A few more choice words were said, but otherwise they both went *to opposite sides of the bar and did not speak to each other the rest of the night.*

Now they have ruined a perfectly good evening for me because I don't know what I'm supposed to do. I'm the manager! I'm supposed to know what to do. Why didn't I break up the fight? Big Bob is not their manager, now what do I do? I have two salesmen who now hate each other, and we have another full day of meetings tomorrow.

Back at the hotel, I decided to call Dad for his opinion. This had to have happened to him before, and he would have the solution. I told the long, dragged out story about how the fight emerged. Following this, Dad said, "Yes, so what?" I replied, "So what do I do about this? I'm the manager!"

Conflict occurs every day in organizations, and some of it is actually good. In fact, the literature distinguishes functional conflict, that which can move the organization forward, from dysfunctional conflict, or that which is not in the best interest of the organization.

Functional conflict can help generate new ideas, mend relationships, or be the catalyst for major organizational changes. I'm sure we can all recall a time in which a major argument or a fight with a loved one actually improved the situation. The same is true in organizations too. A large body of literature supports the "collaborative" approach to resolving conflict— or looking for solutions in which both sides get what they want. If one side withholds information, or looks out only for themselves, the organization as a whole suffers, and this defines dysfunctional conflict.

A Model for Managing and Resolving Conflict

This model starts by first exploring in depth what the source of the conflict is. We need a clear picture of what is really going on in order to generate effective solutions.

DIAGNOSE
↓
DESIGN A PLAN
↓
ACT
↓
EVALUATE

The second step is to design a plan for resolving the conflict. Often the conflict becomes worse if we act too quickly. Think about solutions, draw upon your past experiences, evaluate the key players, and fine-tune your solution before acting.

The third step is to take action, followed by evaluating whether or not the action worked. Let's examine each step in more detail.

Diagnose

The first step is to find the source of the conflict. When you have a flat tire on your car, you don't solve the problem by changing the oil. Likewise, you wouldn't want to solve a conflict between two people by restructuring the entire organization.

The definition of conflict basically evolved from the motivation model presented in Chapter 3.

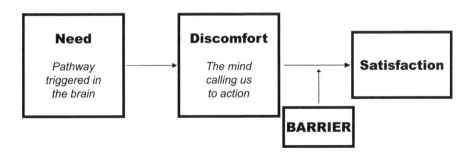

The only difference is that conflict occurs between discomfort and satisfaction, leading to no satisfaction. Let's say I come home from work and the need that is triggered in my brain is that of hunger. That leads to discomfort, and to solve my discomfort, my mind recalls the leftover supreme pizza that I have waiting in the refrigerator from the previous night. My plan is to walk to the fridge and get the pizza, but the barrier in the way is that my wife gave it to the kids for lunch. Conflict can be defined as the goals of one person interfering with the goals of another.

Conflict can occur at various levels within the organization. The first step in the diagnosis is to determine at what level the conflict is occurring.

Level		Example
Structural	——————————→	Re-structure the organization
Inter-Group	——————————→	Changes the dynamic of the group
Inter-Individual	——————————→	Alter the work environment
Intra-Individual	——————————→	Change your thinking

Intra-Individual: Conflict "Inside Your Head"

Intra-individual conflict is conflict that occurs inside our own heads and has no visible behavior attached to it. An example might be the mental processing that occurs when deciding what type of car to buy. I went through this recently. I'd been thinking about this while sitting at my desk, and it was causing problems because I couldn't concentrate on my work.

This reinforces the point that conflict doesn't have to be work related in order for managers to be interested in it. If you are sweating over something unrelated to work, you are not giving work your full attention; therefore, management should care about this.

This also illustrates that conflict doesn't have to have a negative outcome in order to count as conflict. If it takes energy that I could be using in more productive ways, it counts. Many positive things, such as having a baby or building a new house can create high levels of intra-individual conflict.

I decided a few years ago that I was going to abide by the speed limits, as the occasional speeding ticket was getting costly, and I wasn't saving time anyway. I was not a radical driver, but I did like to keep up with the fastest lane of traffic. I made a conscious effort to drive about five miles over the speed limit and to stay in the middle lanes. This, as it turns out, is quite a stressful undertaking in Omaha.

I was on my way to teach an early morning management class when an old pickup truck came right up behind my back bumper (in order to save space, I presume), passed me on the right, then cut in front of me rather quickly, almost clipping my front bumper. This was, of course, to show me that I was holding up the entire world, and he would not have it.

> *I've had a lot of worries in my life, most of which never happened.*
>
> Mark Twain

Now, recalling from Chapter 1, our minds work like a computer, consider the concept of "memories." My favorite, most relaxing place in the entire world is the hot tub at our place in Arizona. The weather is perfect, there is rarely any wind, few clouds, and it is very hot. This hot tub is surrounded by beautiful palm trees, and I'm generally there at the end of the day, after a full day of golfing and being in the sun. There are airplanes flying over, not unlike the ones I dream about owning someday, and I'm truly away from it all, planning such things as where to go to dinner and what golf courses to play the next day.

Think of your favorite place and really imagine it for a few minutes. If you do this, you will find that you can almost put yourself in the state of being there. Try this. Pull from your brain's hard drive the movie of yourself eating the biggest, juiciest dill pickle you can think of. Did you salivate a little bit? I bet you did!

This concept is the basis for much of psychology. Why are we extremely sad at funerals, but not as sad one year later? One explanation would be that, at the funeral, the movie we are playing is about our loss. We are realizing that we will never see or talk to our loved one again and are consumed with how we will cope. One year later, the movies that play in our heads are about the happy times and memories. This is how the mind works. We don't "get over" bad things, we just assign them a different meaning. To add another layer of complexity, our minds are able to easily create these stories and images.

Going back to the morning on the freeway, my mind started creating the movie in which this old pickup truck does, in fact, clip my bumper. I then careen into the next lane, pushing a semi-truck full of gasoline into a school bus full of kids on their field trip to the zoo. The bus turns on its side, explodes, and there are massive injuries, even some deaths, including my own. My kids are now fatherless, and there are 32 students in my 8:00 class who now have the morning free. What was this guy thinking!

Remember, this event did not happen, and I objectively know that this did not happen. The movie I'm creating was not real, but I had the physiological symptoms of anger. I was sweating, had a red face, and my hands were trembling a bit. I got in front of my class and was out of focus the first half hour. All of this over an event that never happened! It was not real; I made it up. This is called intra-individual conflict. How many conflicts do you make up in your head that never happen?

I prefer not to be in meetings with two particular colleagues because they have made me angry at one time or another. I avoid them, and when I have to meet with them, I start playing the movies several days in advance. I will recall what one person said to me, what I should have said in response, and plan for the future attack. I basically end up conducting the meeting in my head three days before it actually happens, creating a worst-case scenario. To make it worse, the meetings usually go fine, and these people have no idea that I feel this way about them.

Here's the problem: Sometimes the movies in our heads lead to real actions or decisions. Several years ago, I had approval to hire a new staff person and was trying to nail down the parameters of the job. I knew I wanted someone of the same caliber and qualifications as "Karen"— someone who performed a similar function in another department. What I did not know was Karen's salary, and this was important information in that I was ready to advertise the position. I asked my immediate supervisor what Karen was making, and he hemmed and hawed and made some excuse that he didn't know, but I also knew that if he wanted to find out, he could do so with a simple phone call.

What follows is a slightly exaggerated transcript of the movie that I created in my head on the way home from work:

Why wouldn't he tell me what Karen makes? I know salary discussions are somewhat taboo in this organization, but this is information I need. It will be a problem if I hire someone and pay them too much, but if I'm too low, nobody will apply. It's not like I really care how much money Karen earns, I just need a benchmark.

I wonder if the reason he wouldn't tell me is that she is making a lot of money? She is pretty good, and I've never heard her complain about money issues like the other staff members. That must be it. She is a high-paid gun, and it must be kept a secret.

You know, she really isn't that good. I mean, she is OK, but why would they pay her so much money that they are afraid to tell me? It must be quite a sum of money, maybe even more than I make.

That is it! Why else would he not tell me? She must make even more than I do. She's not that good. I mean, yes, she has an MBA, but so what? Plus, she would be nothing without her support team. I really can't believe they think she is more valuable than I am.

This is potentially so much more damaging than simply an exaggerated movie in my head. The next day, I might ask other workers what they think Karen makes and, after telling the story, have the whole department thinking that Karen is an overpaid, underperforming, money-sucking drain on the organization. This is real and at that point becomes something well beyond just a movie that I played in my head.

That is why I don't want you to pass this off as some psychological issue to deal with. We *all* play movies in our heads. The key is to manage yourself and your team in such a way that these movies cause minimal interference with what you are asking your team to do.

Inter-Individual and Inter-Group: Conflict Between People

He was a consultant visiting us to see how our business ran and to see if any of his "solutions" could benefit us. I just didn't like him. He used big words and talked in a whiny, nasal voice. Like most consultants, he thought he knew everything about how we should do things.

I had said twice now in this meeting, "I guess we'll have to agree to disagree." This is not how I normally talk!

The next meeting occurred about a month later. Yes, I had been dreading it, but my strategy was simple. Ignore him, and he will go away, so to speak. I knew if I became defensive again, I would get mad, and I was having too good of a week to let him ruin it. It seems as if the others in the meeting had the same strategy, because the guy made a somewhat controversial presentation, and the only people who challenged his assertions were those who were just meeting him for the first time.

This is the type of conflict that can really damage organizations. The conflict was not about this consultant's ideas, but rather it was about his personality. He did not fit in with the rest of the team, and he had a hard time selling his ideas because of the way he came across.

The organization lost out because my colleagues did not hear my ideas or the ideas of the other team members who had a similar strategy to deal with this situation. He could then go to top management and sell his ideas by saying "well, nobody disagreed with me during the meeting."

You may think that this wouldn't happen to you because you are "strong" enough to challenge someone. While true to some degree, the truth is we *all* avoid situations that cause us pain. It's the fundamental law of human behavior discussed in the last chapter.

What do you do when someone makes fun of your religion or tells an off-color joke? Most of us do not say something like, "Hey, that offends me." Instead, we consciously or unconsciously decide to avoid that person in the future.

Inter-individual or inter-group conflict is basically conflict between people because of different personalities. It occurs in every organization, simply because no two personalities are alike.

Structural Conflict

A large portion of conflict is due to the way an organization is designed. Many times, organizations are split into departments with entirely different goals. Consider what the primary objectives are of the following departments:

Sales Department. The goal of a sales department is to maximize dollar sales from the end customer.

Manufacturing Department. The goal of a manufacturing department is to produce quality products efficiently at a low cost.

Accounts Receivable Department. The goal of the accounts receivable department is to keep the number of unpaid accounts low, thereby increasing cash flow and reducing write-offs.

These three departments exist and have to work together in most organizations, but if one department is achieving its goal, it tends to be at the "expense" of other departments. The classic sales versus manufacturing wars tend to revolve around sales thinking that manufacturing is not making what the customers want, and manufacturing seeing an incompetent sales force incapable or unable to sell what is being made.

And when the accounts receivable department makes a push for collecting money quicker, sales go down. Thus, the groups compete, but the primary reason is often structural in nature.

When there is a flaw in the organizational design, conflict is inevitable. This will be given further attention in the next chapter, but understand that sometimes it is not the *people* but rather the *design* of the organization that puts stress on the system. You may, for example, have a manager with so many subordinates that it is difficult to communicate, or you may have rigid rules that are not pleasing to the customer.

Design a Plan

Once you have diagnosed the problem, the next step is to take this information and decide what to do with it. This doesn't necessarily take much time, depending on the conflict, but it is important to make sure you have the information that you need and to generate the correct solution.

Let us now return to my hotel room and my conversation with Dad:

> *"So, what do you want to do, fire both of them?" Dad asks.*
>
> *"No!"*
>
> *"Fire one of them?"*
>
> *"No!"*
>
> *"Ban them from the bar at the next meeting?"*
>
> *I'm getting frustrated now, he is mocking me. "C'mon, just tell me what to do!"*
>
> *"Do nothing. It does not involve you."*
>
> *"Yes it does! I'm the manager."*
>
> *"So what?"*
>
> *"So what! We have a full day of meetings tomorrow!"*
>
> *"If they start slugging each other at the meeting tomorrow, call me!"*
>
> *Great help, Dad.*

Later on I realized that one key principle in conflict management is to know which conflicts to avoid. This is why it is important to step away and look at your options. It takes time to come up with the correct solution, and Dad's solution to leave this conflict alone would not have come to me without stepping away first.

There were many reasons for avoiding this particular incident. First, the incident was not really work-related, other than the initial comment had something to do with sales. There was little to gain by making sure they "liked" one another. Second, they really didn't have to work together.

They were in separate locations and had contact maybe once a year. Finally, it was a conflict that surfaced due to personality differences, so the solution would probably be to make sure they didn't work together, which they didn't.

Managing conflict is a real task in which managers need skills. In fact, one study found that managers spend up to 20 percent of their time managing conflict. That is a significant amount of time when you think that one day out of five is devoted to conflict. It is, therefore, worth your time to decide what is worthy of your attention—and what is not.

Remember the differences between functional and dysfunctional conflict, and that some conflict is actually good for the organization. As noted previously many relationships actually improve because of a good, healthy conflict. People are allowed to vent, new ideas get on the table, and people get off the inertia that often prevents them from truly changing.

The hard part is defining "some conflict." As a rule of thumb, conflict is OK if it does not interfere with the long-term working relationships of the parties. I know it is a vague definition, but so is the concept.

Sometimes conflict will resolve itself simply because of the passage of time. I recall many years ago when a delivery driver made a sarcastic remark to me about the condition of "his" truck after I finished delivering orders in it. It bothered me on multiple levels. One, I always pick up after myself. Two, this was not "his" truck, but, rather, multiple drivers used all trucks depending on the day. I was about ready to engage him in a heated debate when I got distracted by a telephone call. After the call, I could not find him.

The next day, I really didn't care anymore. I realized that I had little to gain by pursuing a conversation about this minor incident. I would keep the incident locked in my head for future reference, but what was there to gain by a confrontation? Having a day to ponder settled this for me, and I now have a personal rule that states that I will not confront an individual until a full day has passed, and I've had time to think about my options.

This does not mean I always cool off. In fact, sometimes pondering the conflict for a day convinces me even more that I'm right. Even then, waiting for a day or so allows me to clearly develop a good strategy for addressing and resolving the conflict.

If you are thinking that the stories in this chapter are "petty," and not really important, how do you think the really large conflicts get started?

Act

If you have done a thorough job of both identifying the source of the conflict, and you have designed an effective plan, then the solution almost comes naturally. The key is to take the resolution seriously. Pick a course of action, and do what it takes to implement it and to show the team you really mean it.

Resolving Intra-Individual Conflict

This concept of conflict was given the most attention in this chapter because, from my perspective, it is the most complicated and probably the largest source of conflict. Our minds are continuously at work processing information, and the important thing is to recognize that we all play and create movies of events in our heads. Most of the time, this allows us to solve problems, but, in other cases, it causes them. The following items can help solve conflict at this stage:

Know your own patterns. Keep a journal of the conflicts that bother you. Then structure your day so that your "trigger" items don't interfere with your whole day. I have one particular project that is long term in nature, and it generally causes conflict because I have trouble getting my way with the people I'm working with. I therefore do not schedule meetings or work on this project early in the day, because I don't want these movies playing in my head for an entire day. I schedule work on this project at the end of the day.

This works for me because I don't take work home with me. If you do take work home with you, this might not be the best strategy. Your family probably gets tired of hearing you vent every night, and this just simply creates another source of conflict in your life.

Know your team. It is hard to know about other people's intra-individual conflicts by definition, but simply being aware of how powerful it is does help. Try to observe during a workday or during a meeting when people seem to be tuning out, and are distracted, cranky, or otherwise nonproductive. Observing comes naturally to many managers, and it is a critical step in minimizing conflict.

Don't "trigger" your team. Don't intentionally create conflict in the hopes that it will make things better. Don't hit them up with a major project during a bad time, or otherwise "push their buttons." When under stress, people behave irrationally, and it rarely has a positive outcome.

Address your patterns. The brain is hard to manage, but it can be done. I do recommend that you create a mental movie of your "stress-free place," such as my hot tub example, and use it. Remember, you are playing these movies anyway; they might as well be good ones. I'm also talking about using this as a tool, as opposed to creating a happy place that will make conflicts go away. Remember, sometimes intra-individual conflict is good in the sense that it points us to solutions.

Resolving Inter-Individual and Inter-Group Conflict

By definition, conflict at this level is due to personality differences, and those are difficult to change. The key is to match up people who naturally work well together, who understand each others' strengths and weaknesses, and who are able to capitalize on these differences. Again, this doesn't mean that anytime people have different personalities and the resulting conflict, they need to be split up. Instead, recognize that if the conflict is ongoing, the people do need to work together, and if talking things out is not working, then sometimes the team needs to be shuffled around.

Start with a meeting and get all the issues on the table about how the conflict is affecting the organization. They may decide to solve the conflict on their own, but in the absence of that, you may need to shuffle projects and duties around in order to keep the parties apart.

The solutions to conflict between groups are similar to conflict between individuals, but you have the added complexities that occur when groups work together. These phenomena can lead to conflict. A few common ones are these:

Groupthink. This occurs when group members want so badly to concur that the norm for consensus overrides almost everything. The Challenger space-shuttle disaster in the 1980s is a commonly used case study in management. There were many people who questioned whether a launch was safe, but the decision was made to go ahead.

Escalation of commitment. This occurs when individuals or groups continue on a course of action that is wrong, despite clear evidence that the action is wrong. This happens primarily when they believe that they are responsible should the course of action fail. By continuing on the wrong course of action, the group or individual avoids having to admit that they made a poor decision.

My very first stock purchase years ago involved a company that was supposedly going to quadruple in price over the next few months. This hot tip came from a successful investor in our community, and I was not going to miss out on this once-in-a-lifetime opportunity. Six months later, the price of the stock was about half of what I paid to purchase it. This successful investor thought this was great news, because now the stock was an even a better bargain! I bought more shares and watched the company eventually go bankrupt. I'm sure the successful investor believed what he was saying, but an outsider would have had a more objective opinion.

Time. One advantage of groups is that more brainpower is used, leading to generally higher quality decisions. However, we must also recognize that groups take more time than individuals to reach decisions. Often we cannot understand what is taking a department so long to do something, when the reality is that it oftentimes can be traced to simple group dynamics.

Divided responsibility. Individuals will make riskier decisions in groups because the responsibility is split up. This can lead to no one person feeling that they are accountable, and certainly conflict occurs and finger pointing takes place when bad decisions are made.

So understand that when working with groups and solving conflict, you have a similar solution set as with the individual level of conflict. However, you add a layer of complexity based upon how groups function.

Resolving Structural Conflict

If you correctly diagnose the conflict as being structural in nature, then something with the nature of how the organization is put together needs to be fixed, and this is the topic for the next chapter. Restructurings are often costly and many times totally turn the organization upside down, which creates a whole array of other types of conflicts.

Your Personal Biases

Recall from Chapter 1 that managers tend to be biased toward what has worked for them in the past (e.g. "If your only tool is a hammer, then every problem looks like a nail.").

For example, my orientation tends to be toward restructuring to solve problems. I like to step back and take a big-picture approach primarily because this worked successfully for me in the past.

Years ago, Dad had his version of the organizational chart along the wall of our conference room. He had simply taken index cards and written each person's name on the card, then pinned them up underneath a header card that had their department written on it. The supervisor was listed first, and the others were listed in the order of tenure. We did not use formal job descriptions, and things like job analysis were not widely used back then. It was not uncommon for people to work in multiple departments.

When the typical problems associated with a growing organization arose, it was easy to find a solution by simply sitting down and analyzing the board until a solution came. He would then jump up, move some cards around, and announce who the new delivery driver was, how the routes would be shifted, and how this would affect the team. It really did work, but it was because the conflicts he was dealing with were structural in nature, again due primarily to growth.

Fast forward a few years to my first days on the job at the branch location. The first thing I did was create my own bulletin board, and it did help with the larger conflicts and the bigger structural issues that this branch location faced.

However, since it worked most of the time, I relied on it too much. When I could not get the drivers to come to work on time, to finish their deliveries, or to get back to the warehouse early, the bulletin board was of no use. That is why it is crucial to go through all steps of the model.

Evaluate

The final step is to assess whether or not your intervention solved the problem. Be careful not to overdo it. It is easy to think that if something worked, more of that something would work even better. I have seen organizations that will add rules and procedures that were needed, but continue to add more and more rules that actually hamper the organizational effectiveness. Remember that taking a higher-than-recommended dose of a medicine does not speed recovery. The same is true of management techniques: More is not necessarily better.

Be careful in the evaluation stage to examine the impact of your resolution on other departments. There is a classic case study in management in which a young accountant reportedly saved a railroad about $200 per year by issuing each train station only one restroom key instead of two. The key would frequently get locked inside the bathroom. To get a replacement key, a form needed to be filled out, and this took time. Because the restroom is a critical part of a train station, the station managers would simply break a window, which constituted an emergency that could be paid out of petty cash. This "cost saving idea" actually cost the company an estimated $20,000 per year!

Remember, some conflict is a natural part of our day-to-day functioning. It can help us overcome inertia, spur us to new market ideas, or energize the team to come up with better solutions to problems. By using the four-step model introduced in this chapter, you can have the tools to better distinguish between "good" and "bad" conflict and have a set of tools ready to assist in solving it.

The Collaborative Model of Conflict Resolution

One of the more popular conflict models classifies the resolution methods into five categories based upon how much you are looking out for your own best interests, as opposed to being concerned about the interests of others. This model is intended to promote the collaborative approach in which both sides get everything they want.

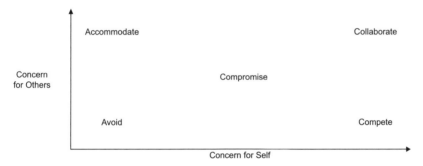

One activity that illustrates this model involves two people at a grocery store who are both trying to purchase the last bag of lemons on the shelf. After arguing over who found the bag first, the grocer sees the only fair solution is to split the lemons, giving each person half. This is a compromise solution, as each side only gets half of what they originally wanted.

Collaboration would have occurred had the parties dug deeper into trying to determine what the other side really wanted. It is revealed later that one wanted the juice from the lemons to make lemonade, and the other wanted the rind from the lemons for pie crust. If they had only taken the time to explore the other side, both would have received exactly what they wanted.

This is an interesting illustration, and a fun seminar activity, but when I reflect on the significant conflicts I have had at work, the solutions rarely involved total satisfaction for both sides. It is, therefore, worth at least considering situations in which the other four resolution methods might be preferred.

Avoidance. Defined as having little concern for either self or others, avoidance is the desired resolution method when you have no interest in solving the problem.

Sometimes the disruption involved with solving a conflict would outweigh the benefits of a resolution. I don't want to call a departmental meeting to find out who left the coffeemaker on overnight, or form a committee to find out where all of the inter-office envelopes are going. Some things are best left alone.

You should also consider whether or not you can solve the conflict. If you really have no chance of changing anyone's mind, this might also be a time to avoid the situation. Also, sometimes you need more information. Little conflicts could be symptoms of much bigger issues, and it does little good to continue to try to solve the symptoms of a problem when a much bigger problem exists.

Accommodating. This method means you are caring about others' needs more than your own. While this may sound compassionate, remember, if you are right, and they are wrong, the organization does not benefit. However, sometimes it is best to "give in." For one thing, if you really are wrong, accommodating shows others that you are reasonable.

I have one person at work who will never give an inch on anything. What she doesn't realize is that conflicts with her are approached differently. I don't think she is reasonable; therefore, I package and present situations totally differently than for someone I consider rational and objective.

You also should consider being accommodating when there are larger issues at stake. Giving in on small items may help you build "social credit" for future issues. Also, sometimes harmony and organizational stability are more important than the conflict itself.

A hard one for managers is to intentionally let people make mistakes so that they learn for themselves. You obviously would want to do a cost-benefit analysis first, but consider the benefit of doing this.

Competing. Competing in this context is caring about your own needs more than others. What I don't like about the definition is that it implies that competition itself can be a negative thing. No, it could simply be that you are right, and the competing style could be the best way to get it done.

Consider, for example, situations in which quick, decisive action is vital. You don't have time to form a committee, gather opinions, or form a task force. Also, you may find yourself in a position where an unpopular decision needs to be made, such as downsizing, budget cutting, and the like. Sometimes it is best to make the decision all alone so that other departments or people don't have to take any blame, like "the buck stops here" approach to management.

You also will find this to be the most effective approach against people who are doing the same thing to you. While collaboration is still preferred, sometimes you have parties that will not do this, and you need to recognize this in advance.

Compromising. This is a good back-up when collaboration won't work. Sometimes you have parties with equal power who are totally committed to their goals. Other times, a temporary settlement is needed, or time pressures warrant a "splitting the difference" approach. Just make sure you remember that a compromise, by definition, only gives each side a partial solution. Don't approach conflict by first deciding to split the difference. Look for the win-win solution first, and then fall back on compromise if you must.

Negotiation as a
Conflict-Resolution Strategy

The word *negotiation* probably makes you think of either haggling for a new car, or a heated labor-management dispute in which managers are trying to stave off a strike. While these certainly are negotiating situations, the principles surrounding proper negotiation actually serve as one basis for resolving conflict.

I'm convinced that most of us recognize this on an intuitive level, but it really became clear to me when I realized my four-year-old daughter was using the principles on me. I was mildly upset that there were toys all over the garage, and I could not get my car inside. The conversation went something like this:

> *Dad: "Ellie, come and pick up your toys in the garage so I can get my car in!"*
>
> *Ellie: "Daddy, can I have some dessert?"*
>
> *Dad: "No Ellie, didn't you hear me? I said you need to pick up your toys in the garage!"*
>
> *Ellie: "First?"*

Wow, she is good! And, yes, she did get dessert, and, as usual, I ended up picking up the toys in the garage. Ah, the power of reinforcement.

To illustrate the principles of negotiation, I like to use the example of buying a car. It is one of the few real negotiation transactions in Western society. My international students point out that in many parts of the world they negotiate for things such as groceries. They are very comfortable with negotiating because they do it frequently. I would guess that buying a car is not on the list of fun tasks for most of us, primarily because we are not comfortable negotiating.

It is time to buy a new car. I know what vehicle I want and proceed to the dealership. The first thing I will find is that the dealer will have a starting point. This is generally the sticker price. I find the sticker on the car I like to be $48,000.

Almost everyone knows that you never pay full sticker for a car. I did have a student who said his wife ran out one day and paid full price for a car. When I asked him why she did this, he said it was out of spite. I'll bet that was a really good argument! Anyway, most of us know we are going to pay something less than the sticker price.

How much less? We don't know this piece of information, but they do. Let's just say that they have been told by their managers that they should not, under any circumstances, sell this vehicle for less than $42,000. This number is called the *resistance point* and is defined as the amount in dollars that one party will not negotiate past.

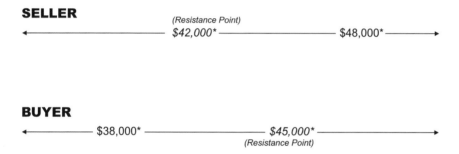

I have it in my head that I would like to get this car for about $38,000. I don't think they will go this low, but after looking at my budget, I've decided that under no circumstances will I pay more than $45,000 for a vehicle. This is my resistance point. Will I purchase the vehicle? To answer this question, you need to determine if a "contract zone" exists. This is done by drawing vertical lines on each resistance point.

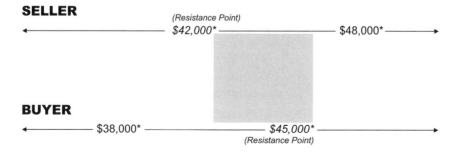

As you can see, the contract zone does exist, and I should purchase the car. The price will be between $42,000 and $45,000.

What if my resistance point is $42,100? In this case, I should get the vehicle, but it will be a tough negotiation. I like framing the negotiation in this fashion because it provides you with a usable framework before you go in. You should create this chart mentally before engaging in any negotiation.

The chart also shows that a negotiation is really all about discovering the other side's resistance point. The salespeople are well trained at doing that. When they ask what you want your monthly payment to be, what you were hoping to get for trade-in, and how much you owe on your existing vehicle, they may simply be trying to uncover your resistance point.

The buyers are doing the same thing by price shopping, doing homework, and maybe finding out what others have paid. Both sides are engaged in activities designed to uncover the resistance point.

The chart also forces you to assess whether or not you are in a negotiation situation to begin with. We often assume that we are not, and pay more than we should, like maybe at a furniture store when the item is negotiable. We also don't want to make the mistake of trying to negotiate when we shouldn't, like at the grocery store. The chart helps us know our limits, for example, when the boss is starting to think we are petty for trying to get a raise. Use the framework to assess your situation before taking any action.

The literature makes a distinction between distribution and integrative bargaining. This distinction closely parallels the collaborative conflict resolution methods discussed previously. In a distributive situation, you are basically negotiating over who gets what amount of some sort of fixed pie. For example, if I negotiate an extra $1,000 off the price of the car, this is then $1,000 less than the dealer receives.

Integrative bargaining occurs when we are truly looking for a collaborative solution. This is ideal but, as discussed, not always possible.

Framing the Negotiation

Often, two different parties will see the same situation in different ways. This has been one theme throughout this book, and it also holds true for negotiations. A *frame* is simply how information is presented.

A number of interesting framing studies have been done over the years. Bazerman and Neale discuss a study in which they handed half of the participants in the experiment the following story:

> You are lying on the beach on a hot day. All you have to drink is ice water. For the last hour you've been thinking about how much you would enjoy a nice cold bottle of your favorite beer. A companion gets up to make a phone call and offers to bring back a beer from the only place nearby where beer is sold: A fancy resort hotel. She says the beer might be expensive and asks how much you are willing to pay. She will buy the beer if it costs as much as or less than the price you say, but if it costs more, she won't buy it. You trust your friend and there is no possibility of negotiating with the bartender. What price are you willing to pay?

The other half of the room received this version of the same story:

> You are lying on the beach on a hot day. All you have to drink is ice water. For the last hour you've been thinking about how much you would enjoy a nice cold bottle of your favorite beer. A companion gets up to make a phone call and offers to bring back a beer from the only place nearby where beer is sold: A small rundown grocery store. She says the beer might be expensive and asks how much you are willing to pay. She will buy the beer if it costs as much as or less than the price you say, but if it costs more, she won't buy it. You trust your friend and there is no possibility of negotiating with the store clerk. What are you willing to pay?

> *Don't take all the money*
> *that's on the table.*
>
> Patricia Fripp

They found that participants were willing to pay a significantly larger amount from the fancy resort hotel ($7.83) as opposed to the grocery store ($4.10). Why is that? Consider the movie that you created in your head as you read the story. When I'm at a fancy resort hotel, two things happen. One, I expect to pay more. Two, I'm probably on vacation, so I will be less sensitive to price.

If you frame the story around a rundown grocery store, a different movie is created. I picture a grocery store at a campground. I've parked the RV and am going to the General Store for firewood, ice, and beer. The mental movie just doesn't involve prices as high as the fancy resort hotel.

The key point is this: How information is presented can have an impact on the resistance points that you set.

Another interesting frame is called the *endowment effect*. It states that humans will place a higher value on something that is already believed to be in their possession. This is one reason why car dealers are so insistent on the test drive. If they can get you to believe or think that this particular car is yours, you will be inclined to pay more. I fell for this a number of years ago, and I knew I would. The dealer told me to take the car home overnight. Well, my wife and I grew attached to the particular vehicle, and the search was over!

I'll bet most of us have "junk" in our basement or in storage that is of little monetary or even sentimental value. We would not purchase these items if we saw them in a store, but we also don't want to sell them. This is partially explained by the endowment effect. The items have value to us simply *because* they are ours.

Kahneman and his colleagues did a study a number of years ago in which part of the subjects were given a coffee mug as they entered a seminar classroom. They were told that it was theirs to keep, but that they could choose to sell it to others in the group who did not receive a mug. Those who did not get a mug were given some money and told they could either keep the money or buy a mug with it. They were asked to write down what they would be willing to pay for the mug. Those who had the mugs were asked what dollar price they would be willing to sell their mugs for.

Those who had the mug chose a median value of $7.12 for the mug, while the potential buyers valued the mug at $2.88. The role that you are in largely determines your reference point, and the research clearly shows that the role of "owner" makes you put a higher value on items.

Hardball Negotiation Tactics

I enjoy discussing the hardball tactics, not so I can use them, but because they illustrate how the human mind processes information. I do not recommend using these techniques. There are ethical issues involved, and frankly most of these take some amount of time to perfect. But be aware of them so they don't get used on you.

Good Guy/Bad Guy

This is where two negotiators on the same side take on entirely different personalities. The bad guy begins by behaving somewhat irrationally, such as throwing a "temper tantrum" or saying something very rude to the other side. He then storms out of the room, leaving the good guy to take over. Although this can lead to concessions and quicker agreements, it is generally difficult to pull off in practice.

The point is either to make the other side feel sorry for the good guy ("I can't believe his personal problems are going to affect my sale to you!") or to rush to close the sale ("Why don't you and I just finish this deal before he comes back in the room?").

I was on a sales call with a team member who prided himself on "telling it like it is." He would sometimes push the envelope with a client, saying their objections were unfounded, or that they really didn't understand the product. This is an application of "good guy, bad guy," because when he went too far and offended the potential client, I could just jump in and say, "Don't mind Bob, he sometimes gets overly passionate about this product. He's not trying to offend you." This worked, because Bob did say what needed to be said with a buffer to smooth things over.

Highball/Lowball

While it is common and recommended to offer less than we think the seller will take, this hardball tactic surfaces when the offer is intended to shift the other side's resistance point. The negative effects of this are that you can come off as looking very unknowledgeable regarding the product or the market, and sometimes the other side may not believe you are serious about making an agreement. So you want to make an offer that is at least on the charts so that you look like you are serious about making an agreement.

When I purchased my first house, I put in an offer that was way too low. The seller declined the offer, so I bumped it up a bit. The second offer was declined as well, so I finally ended up paying the asking price. So, I first gave the impression that I was not serious about making an agreement, but quickly revealed that I was willing to pay any price for this house.

When I sold this property a few years later, the first offer that came in was also way too low. My real estate agent told me we should counter, but I declined, thinking that the person who put in the first offer was not serious. The point is that there is a delicate balance between negotiating and taking yourself out of the game altogether.

Bogey

This occurs when you make the other side believe that an issue that is of little importance to you is actually quite important. Then, when you concede it late in the negotiation, you appear to be a hero to the other side, when, in fact, the issue was not relevant to you. The negative effects of this are that often the truth comes out.

If I'm negotiating the purchase of a new car, I may ask for extras, such as free floor mats or free rust-proofing. If the salesperson agrees to the deal, I'm happy for the moment, but if I later find out that rust-proofing and floor mats are already included in the purchase price, then I don't feel as if I got as good a deal.

The Nibble

The nibble occurs when other items are proposed after the deal is supposedly complete. The nibble tactic takes advantage of the other party who perceives that the negotiation is complete so they will be more likely to give in. The main problem with this is that it often works, but being nibbled could upset the party to the degree that it harms future negotiations.

In a car purchase, I've seen this used when items like documentation fees show up after the negotiation is complete. It is easy to convince myself that it is "only another $89" at this point.

Chicken

This tactic occurs when a large threat is proposed, such as saying, "Agree to this, or we will break off negotiations for good." The problem obviously is when the bluff is called. This will harm the credibility of future statements because the other side doesn't know if it is real or another bluff.

I tried this on a car purchase once just to see if it worked. I told them to come down another $250, or I was heading to another dealer. They called my bluff and brought the keys back to my old car. I had very few options at this point, as I painted myself into a corner. I made up some story about it being too late on a Friday evening for me to continue shopping for a car, and I accepted the original offer. This kind of tactic may be expected at a car dealer, but I'm sure my credibility would be shot had I tried this technique on employees or other situations that require a higher level of trust.

Unseen Authority

You might notice how a car salesman rarely declines your offer himself. He goes into the back room to meet with someone and then will frame his response as if it were not up to him. This is not really hardball like the others. We all tend to do this in some form or another ("I can't go out with you because my grandmother is sick"). I declined a golf invitation last week because I didn't want to play. I told the other party I was going to be with my kids. This is true, but I also engaged in a little bit of unseen authority, as I wouldn't have *had to* be with my kids.

I rarely see these hardball tactics in practice in normal day-to-day operations in organizations. I do think the tactics reveal some keen insight as to how the human mind works, and are worth knowing so that you do not make a bad agreement or agree to something that you otherwise would not.

Final Tips

There really are two types of negotiations. The first involves the car-dealer scenario in which you are negotiating money for something. This could be buying a car, home, or negotiating your salary. It seems as if we almost have a different set of ethical standards in this type of negotiation, much like a poker match where it is acceptable to "bluff" on certain issues. This is OK as long as both sides know the rules. I don't think the car dealers are acting unethically, except when they try to convince us that we are not in a negotiation situation. I actually had one salesman tell me that I shouldn't bother shopping around, because all of the vehicles come from the same factory in Detroit, and all are the same price!

The second type of negotiation relates more to the organizational issues that we face on a daily basis. These principles can actually help us resolve conflict. You can frame many issues in the context of the "buy-sell" line discussed here, and come to agreement. Here are some final tips to help get this done.

Know and Focus on the Common Goals

These are the goals or outcomes both parties agree upon, regardless of the nature of the conflict (for example, quality levels, service to the customer, or "getting out of this meeting!"). Common goals will shift the focus away from the conflict and keep everyone looking at the big picture.

Focus on the Conflict,
Not on the People in the Conflict

It is easy to personalize the issue by pointing out others' weaknesses or shortcomings. Doing this will quickly force the negotiation into a distributive mode. You really don't want this, you need people to make decisions and behave rationally. Also, be careful about criticizing people's traits. You can't change traits, so I really have nowhere to go if my wife says that the one thing she can't stand about me is that I'm too tall. What am I supposed to do about that?

Focus on What Is Fair

People are motivated by fairness and equity, so it is important not to try to implement a solution that is clearly unfair or does not distribute rewards fairly. Don't sacrifice a short-term gain for people realizing later that they have been "had." This is not in your best interest.

Summary of Key Points

- There is functional and dysfunctional conflict in all organizations, and managers need to be able to recognize the difference between the two.
- The first step in solving conflict is to diagnose its source.
- Conflict can occur at many different levels in the organization, including intra-individual, inter-individual, inter-group, and organizational.
- The second step is to step away from the conflict, because time can often be the best solution. Frequently, a higher-quality solution can be found by stepping away for a while.
- The third step is to act on the conflict, which can take on many different forms depending on the source.
- In the act stage, you have a tendency to assume that what will solve a conflict is what solved a conflict in the past, and you need to try to avoid this bias.
- The final step is to evaluate the results of your resolution method.
- Although a collaborative approach to conflict resolution is preferred, the other methods should also be used under certain circumstances: accommodate, avoid, compromise, and compete.
- Negotiation techniques should be used as a conflict resolution method when appropriate.
- Framing, or how information is presented, has a large impact on the outcomes of a negotiation.
- Hardball negotiation tactics should be understood by managers. This will prevent these tactics from being used successfully against them.

Selected References

For more information on the different types of conflict, see A. Amason, "Distinguishing the Effects of Functional and Dysfunctional Conflict on Strategic Decision Making: Resolving a Paradox for Top Management Teams," *Academy of Management Journal*, Vol. 39 (1996), pp. 123-148.

For information about the positive results of conflict, see R. Cosier and D. Dalton, "Positive Effects of Conflict: A Field Experiment," *International Journal of Conflict Management*, Vol. 1 (1990), pp. 81-92.

The study about managers spending up to 20 percent of their time resolving conflict can be found at K. Thomas and W. Schmidt, "A Survey of Management Interests with Respect to Conflict," *Academy of Management Journal*, Vol. 19 (1976), pp. 315-318.

A good source on the overall conflict literature is M. Dunnette and L. Hough, *Handbook of Industrial and Organizational Psychology* (Palo Alto, CA: Consulting Psychologist Press, 1992). See the chapter by K. Thomas, "Conflict and Negotiation Processes in Organizations," pp. 651-717.

The common model used to describe the various conflict resolution methods is detailed in K. Thomas, "Toward Multi-Dimensional Values in Teaching: The Example of Conflict Behaviors," *Academy of Management Review*, Vol. 2 (1977), p. 487.

The studies on framing are from R. Thaler, "Using Mental Accounting in a Theory of Purchasing Behavior," *Marketing Science*, Vol. 4 (1985), pp. 12-13. These were discussed in detail, along with other framing examples, in M. Bazerman & M. Neale, *Negotiating Rationally* (New York: The Free Press, 1992).

The "coffee mug" studies that illustrated the endowment effect are from D. Kahneman, J. Knetsch, and R. Thaler, "Experimental Tests of the Endowment Effect and the Coase Theorem," *The Journal of Political Economy*, Vol. 98 (1990), pp. 1325-1348.

For a detailed discussion of hardball tactics, see R. Lewicki, D. Saunders, and J. Minton, *Negotiation* (New York: McGraw Hill, 1999).

6

Structuring the Organization: How to Manage the Boxes and Arrows

"I understand what you want, but our company policy simply won't allow that!"

*I*t was a shivery, blustery January morning in 1939. William Farner stood numbly, fumbling with his keys in the shadow of a small red brick building on Main Street. When the rusting padlock finally surrendered, he hurried inside and stomped off the snow. Spotting a stove pipe across the empty half-lit bay, he summoned a match from his pocket and brought the ancient oil burner to life.

At the east end of town, Donald Bocken navigated his '36 Ford panel truck deftly through the drifts as the first rays of sunlight invaded the morning sky. Pulling up to the front of the warehouse, he studied the smoke rings rising from the chimney and smiled. He knew the coffee would be ready.

Farner peered through the frost-covered window as Bocken banged the truck door shut and trudged up the snow-packed driveway. As they stood warming themselves beside the stove, the two men lit cigars, then silently raised a steaming toast of freshly brewed coffee. The Farner-Bocken Company was officially open for business.

—From Farner-Bocken Company's 50th Anniversary brochure

Notice what my grandfather and his business partner were *not* doing to get this business started. They did not sit down with a consultant and do a gap analysis. They did not use leadership assessment tools to manage their strengths, or commence with any team-building exercises. They did not craft a mission statement to hang on the conference room wall.

What did they do? I'm guessing they just dug in and started working, saving these kinds of management topics for later. I'm not saying they didn't plan, forecast, assess markets, or do things appropriately; it's just that many topics in management are not a high priority for a start-up business.

One topic that does not fall into that category is the design and structure of the organization. "Boxes and arrows" simply refers to the organizational chart, which shows the levels in the organization, job titles, and who reports to whom. This involves asking and answering questions such as these:

- How many different departments do we need?
- How many layers or levels of management should this organization have?
- How can we communicate better given how different each department is?
- Should we have formal rules in writing, or just deal with situations as they arise?
- Should top managers make major decisions, or should managers in the field have that responsibility?

The design is critical because a flawed structure can handicap even the best manager. Consider the phrase "think outside the box." What does it really mean? I'm sure it was coined by someone who thought there was little creativity in their organization, and they were attributing this to people staying in their "box," or job description.

The problem is that the boxes were created to serve a purpose. It has to be frustrating for managers to be given a detailed job description (their box) and simultaneously be told to "think outside your box." One student told me that maybe the phrase really means "think outside the box but don't act outside your box!"

The Principles Behind Organizing Tasks

While I wasn't around in 1939, here is my vision of what happened in the coming months.

> *With only two managers and a handful of workers, the days and nights became incredibly long, especially since the business was growing rapidly. While both Don and Bill were hard workers, the growth of the enterprise was starting to take its toll. Not only were they stressed out, tired, and getting sick of each other, the customers were also starting to notice a decline in service. Invoices were priced wrong, the wrong candy products were getting shipped, and deliveries were running late. They lost several key customers because of these mistakes, which turned out to be the catalyst for some major structural changes.*
>
> *Bill and Don sat down and decided they could no longer run a company in this way. They had too many people doing too many things, and the result was chaos. Everybody doing everything was fine during the start-up phase of this business, but the time had come to organize the business in a better fashion.*

Functional Structure: The Starting Point

The first formal structure that usually emerges is a functional structure. Tasks are divided and organized into departments based upon the logical functions of the organization. This makes one department responsible for a certain set of related tasks. In this case, the structure probably looked similar to the illustration here.

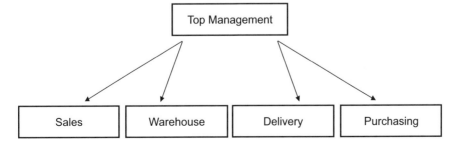

This structure is created without having to add a huge amount of staff, but it requires organizing the functions properly.

The simple functional structure has its advantages. First, it facilitates learning for employees as they work closely together with those in their department and become more specialized. Salespeople can focus on selling and learn "best practices" from each other. Another advantage is that each department is now accountable. Such accountability should reduce the number of errors that occur in the system.

Integrating Between Departments

While everyone agreed that this structure was necessary, it has changed the work environment quite a bit. For example, Don is now in charge of the salesmen, but he misses the warehouse environment. He enjoyed processing orders, boxing things up, and loading them onto the truck. There was just something satisfying about filling a customer's order correctly.

Cy, the warehouse manager, is having similar feelings. He used to get out on the road and talk to customers. Now that he is in charge of the warehouse, he often goes home at the end of the day without ever having looked outside. The rows and rows of candy are starting to get really boring. He misses the good old days when everyone just jumped in where they were needed.

Plus, these changes have created conflict. The organization didn't have as many "territorial" issues until this change was made. Don got mad at Cy this morning because they were running low on Hershey candy bars. Cy blamed Don for selling so many without giving him a heads up. These kinds of things just didn't happen in the old days.

The downside of a functional structure is that each department has a narrow focus, which makes it easy to ignore the needs of the other departments. This narrow focus leads to communication and coordination problems. The solution is to implement mechanisms to assist with the communication and coordination.

The following are some common mechanisms that organizations can use to try to reduce some of the problems that any formal structure creates.

Hierarchy of Authority. Integrates people and functions by specifying reporting relationships.

Direct Contact. Requires managers from different functions to meet to coordinate activities.

Liaison Role. Assigns a particular manager the responsibility of coordinating with managers from other subunits.

Task Forces. Creates a temporary cross-functional committee to solve a temporary problem.

Teams. Requires managers from different functions to meet regularly to coordinate activities.

Integrating Roles. Creates a new role to coordinate the activities of two or more functions or divisions.

Integrating Departments. Establishes a new department to coordinate the activities of functions or divisions.

The complexity and cost of these mechanisms increases as you go down the list. The challenge therefore is to establish a level of integration that is appropriate for the problems that exist.

In a restaurant, we create separate functions for cooking food and serving food. These two departments, while separate, also clearly have to work together to give the customer a satisfactory dining experience. What type of integrating mechanism do we use to coordinate the functions in these departments? In a small diner, it might be as simple as identifying the proper reporting relationships, such as informing the cooks that the wait staff has final authority over customer service issues.

Consider a more complex food-service business, like one that specializes in large banquets or wedding receptions. They may need an integrating role such as a supervisor whose sole duty is to coordinate the activities between the cooks and the wait staff.

If the integrating mechanism is too simple, the coordination problems will not get solved. Likewise, if the mechanism is too complex, resources are wasted. Consider what would happen if the small diner created an entire department to coordinate activities.

Other Structure Types

A pure functional structure does not always address the needs of the organization. Recall from the opening story that the functional structure was created because the organization was specifically encountering coordination issues between functions. This is not always the case. Sometimes, the source of the problem can be because of different types of products, different types of customers, or geographical issues.

Product Structure

This approach should be used when coordination problems exist because of the nature of the products. Farner-Bocken later expanded its product line into the wholesale food distribution market. The coordination problems that existed at that point could have been due to different procedures for each type of food.

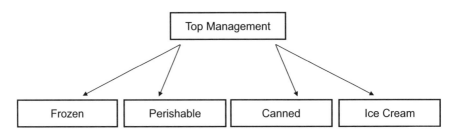

The original functional structure had all of the buyers in the purchasing department. This worked well until the new food products were added. Now, a buyer in this organization would need a separate set of skills for each product line. Purchasing perishable foods, such as lettuce and tomatoes, requires a keen insight into how much product is needed for a given week in order to satisfy customer orders without throwing away rotten products.

The buyer of canned foods, however, is often faced with the challenge of when to take advantage of a discount. Should she purchase a truckload at a discount, or would storage costs eat up the profit?

If this were the only substantial difference, then, yes, we could just train buyers in the various buying methods. But, in this case, it is not just the purchasing function that requires its own skill set. The products are stored differently, with some in temperature-controlled freezers and others on pallets. The produce buyers have to work closely with the sales department to insure fresh product. The delivery drivers need to know how to handle frozen food. It is shipped in a separate compartment on the trucks and requires special equipment and handling.

Each product line has to function as its own little business in this case. A simple functional structure with buyers in their own department would not solve any coordination problems, hence, a product structure is the most efficient.

Market Structure

A market structure is used when an organization has a product line that is used by different customers in different ways. When purchasing a PC as an individual, I may want to go to a Web site, click on various options, and have the computer delivered to my home. If I'm buying for my business, I need a different level of service. I might need to create a network, hook up printers, scanners, and faxes, and integrate my system with the home office. Yes, the product is basically the same, but the question of how to serve the customer is different with different customer types. Thus, a computer retailer may create a "business division" for business customers.

Another example is a restaurant that specializes in banquets and large group events. They consistently serve steak dinners to groups of 100+ people, and the meal needs to be hot and of high quality. They are able to do this because they have a market structure designed for large groups.

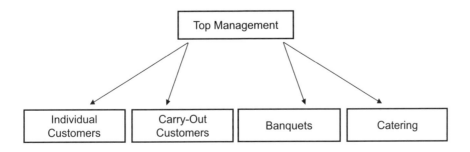

The "individual customer" department has a traditional functional structure with a full menu and traditional service. For a banquet or a large wedding reception, the customer requires an entirely different type of service, which calls for a different type of structure. For a banquet, your choices are "chicken or steak." The wait staff will not ask you what type of dressing you would like on your salad or how you would like your steak cooked.

The food is staged in large institutional oven warmers. They don't wait for you to finish your salad before bringing your entrée. They know how to serve large groups effectively, but simply would not be able to provide equal levels of service to both customer types without two different structures.

Geographic Structure

Sometimes, the coordination problems are caused by geographic barriers. Consider a human resource department for a large organization, which has operations in various parts of the world. They may need entirely separate divisions, assuming that the functions and tasks that they are charged with vary in different locations. For example, HR laws and procedures are different in Kansas City versus Tokyo. This may require an entirely separate department because there would be few synergies associated with working together.

Different locations, in and of themselves, do not warrant a geographic structure. Because the McDonald's restaurant has similar procedures worldwide, I'm sure they don't have a different department for each geographic region. Again, examine where the coordination problems exist and design accordingly.

When the Wrong Structure Is Used

Let's create a hypothetical Chinese restaurant but design it around a very inefficient product structure.

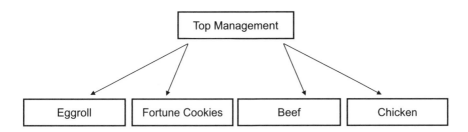

What would a dining experience be like in this structure? Well, you would have a separate staff for each department. If you ordered an egg roll, stir fry beef, and a fortune cookie, these food items would come on three different checks (one from each department), and on three different plates. I'm sure the kitchen would be chaos, with cooks from each department fighting for space on the grill. Even if this restaurant had excellent food, it would be bankrupt in a short time with so many extra layers of management.

This may seem like an extreme example, but I'm convinced that many organizations wallow in an ineffective structure, costing them untold millions of dollars.

Years ago at a family reunion, I was charged with the task of picking up food from one of our favorite little Mexican restaurants. We were expecting about 30 people. The restaurant was one of those places where you order at a window and pick up your food when they call your number. I placed our large order for something like 20 tacos, 15 enchiladas, 25 Mexican fries, and 12 desserts, paid my $175, and proceeded to take a seat with my ticket-number in hand.

A short time later I noticed the line at the window was not moving, and customers seemed to be getting cranky. At one point, I heard the cashier say, "It's not our fault. The guy over there just placed a $175 order!"

The food was great, but they just were not structured to handle a large order like mine and at the same time satisfy their typical customer. If they have a need to handle both customer types, they could purchase a second cash register so that the regulars don't have to wait in line. They could also have a different menu that caters for large orders. They could also encourage customers to call ahead of time, or even offer delivery service.

However, if large orders like mine are rare, they would be adding these systems unnecessarily and at a large cost. I know it sounds simple and common sense when discussing a restaurant, but I'm sure you have departments that do not run efficiently simply due to structural issues.

Remember the rule: Look at where the coordination problems exist, and structure the organization accordingly.

The Principles Behind Reporting Relationships

To this point, we have been looking at the principles behind dividing tasks, or designing the organization from "left to right" on the organization chart. The other major design component involves structuring the organization "up and down," or analyzing the hierarchy and the reporting relationships.

An organization's hierarchy emerges when the organization grows to a point at which it needs more layers to operate effectively. We don't just "add people," because these people need to be organized and managed. But managers need to be aware of the natural tendency of organizations to add people unnecessarily.

One researcher discovered that, over a four-year span, the British Navy decreased its number of ships in operation by 68 percent, but the number of dockyard personnel increased 40 percent and top management increased by 79 percent.

Why do things like this happen? Part of the reason is that managers are rewarded for having large departments, either through access to a larger budget, more status, or more power. Another explanation could be that "work expands to fill the time available."

This results in what is called a "tall" organization. A tall organization has many levels of management relative to its size, as opposed to a "flat" organization where the number of managers between the bottom and the top is relatively few. An organization that is too tall will tend to have communication problems. Why? Because the necessary communication has to go through too many levels, resulting in a time delay. Also, with more people involved, the original message tends to get distorted.

How can an organization avoid becoming too tall? One way is by increasing the manager's span of control, which is the number of subordinates a manager directly manages. This, of course, cannot just be done automatically, but, rather, a host of factors will determine how many subordinates one manager can effectively manage.

Span of control is limited by the complexity and the interrelatedness of the tasks. If you are a scientist managing a team that is trying to cure a disease, you may only be able to effectively manage three or four people. If you have an assembly line in which things generally run smoothly, and you are just there to assess problems, then you might be able to manage 100 people without difficulty.

Another key factor detailed in the following section is whether decisions are made more at the top of the organization versus at the bottom.

> *If you don't do it excellently, don't do it at all. Because if it's not excellent, it won't be profitable or fun, and if you're not in business for fun or profit, what the hell are you doing there?*
>
> Robert Townsend

When decisions are made at the bottom, less direct managerial supervision is needed. Also, in a formalized structure, rules dictate procedures, thus largely eliminating the need for managers to make decisions.

Formal Rules and Decision Making

As the vendor that provided candy for a major grocery store chain, we often worked closely with the store managers when the executives from headquarters were in town to tour the stores. It was a great time to meet the executives but also quite a bit of work because we tried to have the candy aisles in perfect shape, which is hard to do with customers around.

The executive team from New York will visit every retail store location and give it the "white glove" treatment. I guess it makes them feel important, but I have to wonder if it really does any good. After all, the tour is announced well in advance. Wouldn't a secret shopper program really show them what goes on in the store? I guess that is not my decision, my job as the candy vendor is to make sure that the candy aisle is flawless. I am at the last store of this tour, and things look good. Nothing is out of stock, dusty, open, or otherwise out of place, so I head home for the evening.

The next morning I received a phone call from a very upset supervisor. The head merchandiser discovered a pricing error on two different candy bars, and they have been selling them for below cost. This is a problem, because I am responsible for getting the store managers the correct price. They later determined that this was a one-time data entry error and didn't cost them much money. However, the team decided that because of this error, all candy-buying decisions would now be made by the head buyer in New York. This has the store manager shaking his head because how can a buyer in New York know the buying habits of people in Sioux City, Iowa?

As it happened, the merchandiser in New York discovered another "error." It seems that a top 10 candy bar was not included in this store's offering. However, a related type of bar, Twin Bing, was on the store shelves and in a prime location no less, even though it was not even in the top 50 for national sales. A few more errors like this, and management was seeing its wisdom in centralizing such important decisions.

What the New York buyers failed to realize was that Twin Bings are manufactured in Sioux City, Iowa, and the factory was right down the street from this grocery store. Yes, on the national level, the competing bar had better sales, but not in this particular store. The store manager is up in arms about this, but since the product decisions are no longer made at the store level, the manager has no control.

A centralized organization is one that has top-level managers making the most important decisions. This has advantages in that it is easier to keep the organization focused on its goals. The downside is that upper-level managers may ignore important decisions because they are focused on making day-to-day decisions.

A decentralized organization has managers at all levels making important decisions. The advantages of this are that it results in high flexibility and responsiveness, and it motivates managers to perform well, because they now have "skin in the game." It is hard to criticize top management when you have the authority to do things your own way. The downside is that planning and control can be difficult.

Formalization Versus Mutual Adjustment

One item on my "to do" list for the day was to return a rented video. While at the store, I decided that I needed another movie to watch on the treadmill to keep me motivated. I found a classic five-day rental and threw it in the back seat of my car. When I went home, my wife ran some errands in my vehicle. Seeing a video in the back seat of the car, she thought I had simply forgotten to return it, so she dropped my freshly rented video in the return slot.

I naively thought that I could simply go back to the store and explain to them what happened. I even thought it was kind of funny that a five-day video rental would get returned 30 minutes after being checked out. They did not see the humor and told me there was nothing that they could do. The video was already scanned back in and put back on the shelf.

My first thought was to bite the bullet and spend another $3 on the movie. After all, I had more to do than argue with an assistant manager about the rules that his headquarters so brilliantly created. Then, it occurred to me that since I had chosen a career of studying and being able to navigate my way around organizations, it certainly would shoot all of my credibility if I couldn't get my way in this situation, so I pressed on.

I finally did get my way after about a 20-minute discussion with a manager. I had to fill out a form and tell them what happened in writing. Although this did make me feel like a criminal, I got my way!

This is an example of an organization with a high level of formalization. Relying on rules has advantages, including consistent levels of service, shorter training times, and a more efficient operation. The other end of the spectrum is called mutual adjustment, which simply means that the team adjusts to each other as the situation changes.

I'm not blaming the video store for my unusual dilemma, but rather use this example as a good illustration of the negative side of formalization. It does not allow flexibility for unusual customer requests, like mine. Again, the positive side in this case is that it shortens training time. They don't have to train managers to make decisions because the rules are in place. They may want to re-think how formalized they are if situations like mine are common, but, if not, they probably come out OK with this level of formalization.

The main point with all of these structural concepts is that an organization must have a structure that fits its unique situation. A custom furniture maker probably shouldn't rely heavily on rules and procedures. On the other hand, an airline captain or a nuclear power plant probably should follow written rules and procedures.

Pulling It All Together: Mechanistic Versus Organic

	Mechanistic	**Organic**
Specialization	Individuals are very specialized (assembly line)	Individuals work together (software development)
Integrated Mechanisms	Simply integrating mechanism (hierarchy well-defined)	Complex integrating mechanism (teams and task forces)
Decision-Making	Very centralized	Very decentralized
Formalization	Driven by rules - standardized	Driven by mutual adjustment

All of these variables combined can be classified into two different types of structures, mechanistic or organic. A mechanistic structure is designed to make people behave in a predictable manner. It is designed around workers specializing in one highly specific task, having a clear hierarchy of authority as an integrating mechanism, centralized decision-making authority, and a large dependence on rules.

An organic organization is just the opposite. Employees work together on a variety of tasks and don't specialize in one particular thing. Complex integrating mechanisms, such as task forces and teams, are used to coordinate activities. Decisions are decentralized, and rules and procedures are minimal. This structure encourages flexibility and decentralized decision making. Roles are loosely defined. Integrating mechanisms are more complex and rely heavily on the use of teams to coordinate among departments.

> *Technology does not run an enterprise. Relationships do.*
>
> Patricia Fripp

Which structure is better? The answer depends on a host of other variables, but most workers probably would not enjoy the pure mechanistic structure. It conjures up images of a classic assembly line in which you are to do what you are told, decisions are made at the top, and any question you have about procedures can be looked up in a book. It seems boring and unchallenging, and it can be.

Why then would an organization want to structure itself this way? Mechanistic means mechanical, so, to use an analogy, picture the engine on your car. Even the biggest SUVs are quite efficient when you consider what you can do with them. I can transport my entire family clear across town on a measly gallon of gasoline, which is mighty impressive.

So what type of "structure" would a car engine have if it were an organization? The "departments" would be things like the fuel system, the oil system, and the transmission. Each one has a specific role to play in getting my family across town. They must do their role without much variance in how the job is done. For example, the oil department can't decide that, instead of oil, it is going to try to lubricate the parts by using water. What would happen? The entire system would literally break down.

The mechanical structure is the most effective structure when the goal of the organization is efficiency without exception or creativity. This is the only way the engine can do its job.

Organic, on the other hand, implies flexibility and adaptability. I think of the human body and its ability to adapt to changing conditions as a system. When we sprain our ankle, we are able to limp to get around. When we are hot, we sweat. When someone threatens us, we have systems in place to fight back. Charged with the same task of getting a family across town without the aid of a car, a human could adapt and find a way to do it. When a car has a breakdown, it cannot fix itself and adapt.

Have you ever tried to stop an ant from completing its task? This is kind of fun. Put a rock or a stick or a leaf in its path and watch what happens. They always find a way around the obstacle. That is organic. It may not be the most efficient, but when creativity is needed, or obstacles can't be predicted, a system needs to be in place that allows for incredible amounts of flexibility.

Contemporary Topics in Organizational Structure

I've used the *Organizational Theory* textbook by Gareth Jones for a number of years now in my MBA courses and have revised the instructor's manual for him on the last couple of editions. Most of the concepts in this chapter have evolved from his ideas. I started using his edition that was published in 1993.

At that time he discussed an emerging structure called the "network" or "boundaryless" organization. The basic premise was that organizations would network with one another, with each organization specializing in one very narrow part of the task or the end product. This results in a blurring of the boundaries between each organization, as it appears to operate as one coherent unit.

I worked in the payroll department of our wholesale business while I helped implement an automated time-clock system. I remember being excited about how much money the company would save. Instead of having 10 different payroll clerks at each branch location manually adding up hours each week, this system would send the tabulated hours over the telephone to a central PC, eliminating both the labor and the chance for error. I marveled at how in the "old days" prior to computers, it took probably 20 people to process payroll. We had this down to about three now, and I was high on this new technology.

Now, there are organizations that will process the entire payroll function for an organization, creating even more efficiencies. What if this is true for other departments within any organization? Could, for example, McDonald's benefit by outsourcing its drive-through window?

Yes, they are actually doing that. There is a call center in Colorado Springs that handles the drive-through window for a chain of McDonald's stores in Missouri. When you pull up to the drive-up window to place an order, your voice is actually traveling through high-speed data lines to the call center. Someone takes your order and in effect emails the order back to the store along with a photo of you in your car. This has cut the drive-through time significantly and reduced the number of complaints about the orders. Talk about technology changing organizations! Some restaurants even have phones with credit card readers on the tables inside. You sit down, place your order, pay, and the food arrives.

This story and others are detailed in Friedman's book, *The World Is Flat*. I discuss his perspective in the final chapter, but, for now, remember that the organizational structure is a key component in the success of an organization.

Summary of Key Points

- How an organization is structured and designed is as important as any other management topic. Without an effective system, nothing will work well.
- Horizontal differentiation involves how to divide and split up tasks.
- Tasks should be split up and coordinated based on where the coordination problems exist.
- Vertical differentiation involves designing the hierarchy and reporting relationships.
- Decision making can either be centralized or decentralized depending on the needs of the organization.
- Organizations must decide how formal to make the rules and procedures. High levels of formalization, while very efficient, also make it hard to handle customer exceptions.
- Structural categories can be summarized into the mechanistic versus organic framework.
- Technology has allowed the proliferation of network organizations that each specialize in one narrow task.

Selected References

A good overview of the challenges of designing an organization is the textbook by G. Jones, *Organizational Theory, Design, & Change* (Upper Saddle River, NJ: Prentice-Hall, 2006).

Details on the various integrating mechanisms can be found at J. Galbraith, *Designing Complex Organizations* (Reading, MA: Addison Wesley, 1973).

Details about Parkinson's Law are in C. Parkinson, *Parkinson's Law* (New York: Ballantine Books, 1964).

For more details on the concept of standardization and mutual adjustment, see H. Mintzberg, *The Structuring of Organizational Structures* (Englewood Cliffs, NJ: Prentice Hall, 1979).

For a classic piece on mechanistic and organic structures, see T. Burns and G. Stalker, *The Management of Innovation* (London: Tavistock Publications, 1961).

Details on network organizations are at C. Snow, R. Miles, and H. Coleman Jr., "Managing Twenty-First Century Network Organizations," *Organizational Dynamics*, Vol. 20 (1992), pp. 5-20.

T. Friedman detailed the McDonald's outsourcing story in *The World Is Flat: A Brief History of the Twenty-First Century* (New York: Farrar, Straus, and Giroux, 2006).

7

Change Management: Effective Leadership During Times of Change

"That is just not the way we do things around here!"

I was at our headquarters for a quarterly sales meeting. At lunchtime, I decided to go over to my grandparents' house for lunch. Grandpa still came to the office about every day and tried to keep up with all of the changes the business was going through, but he generally left the day-to-day management up to others.

He asked me how the meeting was going, and I told him that the most exciting opportunity was to sell sunglasses to convenience stores. The salesman from the sunglass company had made an excellent presentation, the product quality was high, the margins were incredible, and it was easy for the salespeople to order.

Grandpa shook his head with sort of a disgusted look and said, "It will never work."

"Why not?" I asked.

"Did you see how many sunglasses we tossed in the dumpster last year after inventory? These programs just don't fit into our system."

"No, this is different than our other program. This company is guaranteeing the sale!"

"It still won't work."

"Yes it will, you watch!"

I wasn't trying to disrespect his 50+ years of experience in the wholesale distribution business, but I was a bit perplexed as to how he could have *such a strong opinion without attending the meeting. This was a no-brainer. Little investment, existing market, high margins, what else could you want?*

Grandpa clearly needs to learn to change with the times.

The Speed of Change Today

Change has long been a popular management topic although application of change management has certainly taken on different forms over the years. Consider the farming industry, for example. In the 1890s, about 90 percent of the population was employed in agriculture-related jobs. That number is about 2 percent today. Clearly, over the course of 100+ years, many people lost their jobs and were forced to enter a different industry. Remember the farm crisis in the 1980s? Consider the following lyrics from John Mellencamp:

Four hundred empty acres that used to be my farm
… The crops we grew last summer weren't enough to pay the loans
Couldn't buy the seed to plant this spring and the
Farmers Bank foreclosed

What happened to the farming industry? Basically technology improved across the board, from tractors instead of horses, to better seed, fertilizer, combines, and other upgrades. Didn't this industry go through downsizing? Yes, of course, but the difference is that it took over 125 years for the farmers to be downsized. This is a very bad thing if it is happening to you, and I don't wish for farmers to lose their farms (or any business for that matter). But if you examine it from a macro-perspective, you get a different picture. If farmers made up 90 percent of the population in the 1890s, then it took nine out of 10 of us to grow food for 10 out of 10 of us. How many of us would like to return to those days?

As technology improved, the next economic wave was under way: the Industrial Revolution. Economies moved from agrarian based to those dependent on machines. With the advent of the automobile, companies that made such items as "buggy whips" experienced severe economic problems. Sometimes, no matter how efficient your organization is, how well you manage, or how fair or affordable your price, people just don't want the product. Think of the drastic changes that buggy whip makers must have gone through as the automobile replaced horses.

The 1970s saw a shift to more of an information-based economy. Futurist Alvin Toffler calls these changes "waves" or "revolutions" in the sense that they totally changed our way of life. He reflected on how the lives of English villagers were changed as the economy moved from agriculture to factories.

Consider how the information wave changed the lives of blue-collar workers. Technology eliminated many jobs, but also created many more opportunities for those ready to embrace change. Again, it is not a good thing if it is happening to you, but it is reality, and it has been occurring for some time now. Consider Billy Joel's 1980s hit, "Allentown," which was about the steel mills closing down.

> *… we're waiting here in Allentown*
> *For the Pennsylvania we never found*
> *For the promises our teachers gave*
> *If we worked hard*

Just as the Industrial Revolution destroyed the careers of hundreds of thousands of farmers and crafts-workers, the information revolution did the same thing to blue-collar workers during the 1970s and 1980s. In the field of management, gurus such as Tom Peters were discussing concepts like "speed," and how rapidly things were going to change in this new economy.

By definition we don't know what wave is next, but clearly no industry is immune from systemic changes. The very first college course that I taught was a computer class at a community college in the early 1990s. It was an introductory class for Lotus 1-2-3 for DOS, and also WordPerfect for DOS. Remember all the neat menu bar commands, like "shift-F7-1"to print in WordPerfect? In a short time, Windows became popular, and over the course of a few years, the skills that I had previously developed became totally worthless in the marketplace. My point is, this happened over the course of a few years; changes since then have come even quicker.

In his book, *The World Is Flat*, Thomas Friedman discusses what he calls the "triple convergence," which could arguably be the start of the next revolution. He discusses how many of the technological changes that have been around for a decade or more are dramatically changing our world as the technologies start working together, and as people and systems become comfortable with the technology. He notes that computer technologies did not immediately increase productivity because of the time lag involved in getting everyone to use them, use them correctly, and integrate them with other technologies.

He discusses how the light bulb, invented in 1879, was not an immediate hit because of the fact that the whole way of manufacturing and doing business had to change too, and this takes time. You can't just scrap a steam-engine system overnight. In fact, it took almost 50 years for electricity to penetrate 30 percent of households. The same is true of any technology. The systems need to catch up with the technology before they become widely implemented. However, the speed of implementation today is much different. It only took about seven years for the Internet to penetrate 30 percent of American households.

Consider such things as email. In a university environment, we were one of the early adopters of that technology in the mid 1990s. At that time, relatively few people used email so it was almost an internal system to communicate with each other and with the few students who had it.

Today, almost everyone uses email in some form, and because it passed the "tipping point" some years back, the uses and results are phenomenal.

In addition to sending messages back and forth to my colleagues, I can also get email updates from various airlines regarding discount airfares. I can send photographs of my kids to my mother. Even better, I can upload my photos to a Web site, order prints, and she can pick them up at her hometown department store. Just this morning, I got notification from General Motors that my oil was ready to be changed, and another email from the Nebraska Golf Association notifying me of my new handicap.

With Southwest Airlines, I can now print my boarding pass from the comforts of home. As Friedman notes in his book, "In Globalization 1.0, there was a ticket agent. In Globalization 2.0, the e-ticket machine replaced the ticket agent. In Globalization 3.0, you are your own ticket agent."

Change is happening faster than ever, but if you really look at what is going on today, the technological revolution involves so much more than simply "speed." The systemic changes in our economy are quickly changing the role of the modern manager. That being said, the underlying principles around leading people through change have remained constant. In other words, change is change, although the application of this concept is constantly "changing."

Lewin's "Force Field" Model of Change

In the 1950s, Curt Lewin introduced a simple model that illustrates how organizations change. It also shows that we were talking about change management over a half-century ago.

Force-field analysis looks at the forces that are driving change and those that are holding it back. There are always forces in an organization pushing change, such as a maverick manager or new technologies. At the same time, there are opposing forces resisting the change, such as a formal structure, or people who simply won't embrace a new technology. When the "forces for" change are greater than the "resistances to" change, then change will occur.

The status quo is an equilibrium state. To move from this equilibrium, either the forces for change must increase or the resistances to change must decrease.

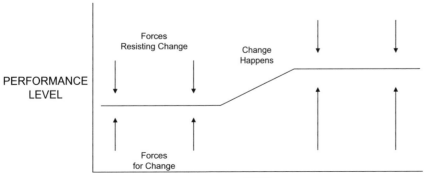

Forces for Change

Most of the forces for change can be attributed to technological changes. Technology drove globalization, which synergistically changed the entire economy. We still occasionally see a politician talking about the North American Free Trade Agreement (NAFTA) or keeping American jobs at home, but the truth is that globalization has already happened, and keeping American jobs at home is not as simple as "buying American." Consider the auto industry. BMW is now producing cars in South Carolina. Ford makes cars in Canada and Mexico.

The global economy has changed the nature of how we compete. "Being better" used to simply mean having a better product, better service, or the best-tasting hamburger. Today, it means being able to stay ahead and creative on multiple fronts, and being able to change quickly is vital to sustaining any real long-term advantage. The Internet has largely eliminated geographic barriers in marketing education products. It is not unusual for me to teach an online class to students from Thailand, Brazil, Europe, and the United States.

In addition to the competitive environment, the global economy has created a highly diverse workforce, requiring managers to be much more flexible in their management style. This requires an in-depth understanding of cultural differences. An organization no longer has the option to say, "Do it our way or leave." There are too many talented people who *will* leave.

In addition, ethics has risen to the forefront of management because decisions must be made much quicker than in previous decades. And, with organizations under much more scrutiny, an ethical misstep can cause bankruptcy, as Arthur Anderson and Enron quickly learned.

Forces Resisting Change

At the same time, there are also forces resisting change. The competitive environment of the auto industry changed dramatically during the 1970s. Remember when Detroit was cranking out the huge sedans? The quality was simply quite low by today's standards. My dad drove Ford LTDs. I can remember when going through the car wash, I had to slide to the middle to keep from getting soaked, and this was with the windows up! Also, we traded cars every few years because they simply didn't last very long. At 60,000 miles it was time to trade in the car.

I'm not picking on this industry; electronics, appliances, and other consumer goods went through the same revolution, but when talking about how organizations and individuals resist change, do you remember what our first response was when the fuel-efficient Hondas and Nissans starting showing up in America?

The initial response was a campaign to "buy American." No, let's not look at our product quality and why anyone would want a Honda Accord instead of a Ford LTD, but rather, let's market the American worker. It just didn't work, and the industry was revolutionized for the better because of it. Chrysler, on the verge of bankruptcy, shifted to the K-car; Ford started designing cars like the Taurus; and the entire industry, including the consumer, benefited. There was resistance at first, but it was overcome by the force of competition.

Resistance to change occurs at both the individual and organizational levels.

Individual Resistance to Change

We all develop habits and routines in our lives. In the classroom, I find that most students always sit in the same desk. If I ask students to stand up and move to a different chair in the classroom, it makes them mildly uncomfortable. Try sitting somewhere other than your normal seat in church. Most of us would like to return to our "own" seats as soon as we could.

> *Never underestimate your power to change yourself; never overestimate your power to change others.*
>
> H. Jackson Browne

Changes generally mean ambiguity and uncertainty, which is obviously not as comfortable as the known. Although it might be exciting to try a new restaurant for a change, most individuals dislike having the same ambiguity and uncertainty when it comes to their careers.

Also, for most of us, our jobs define what our lifestyle is. We simply get used to a certain level of income or certain benefits, such as flextime.

The typical organizational change has a level of uncertainty. People just don't know if things will work out for them personally if downsizings or restructurings are in the future, so it is normal to resist this type of change.

There is some psychology at work. Recall from Chapter 1 that individuals tend to selectively process information due to the complexity of the human mind. This often results in people hearing what they want to hear, or ignoring information that challenges the world they have created.

Organizational Resistances

Resistance at this level is about how the system is designed. You can have people motivated to change, but if the system is not allowing it, it will not happen. One case study I use in the classroom involves the 3M organization. They rely on creativity to sustain their growth, as evidenced by such innovations as Post-it Notes. I could argue whether or not 3M is just simply better at hiring more creative scientists and engineers, but the truth is that they actually "do things" to foster this creativity.

A CEO can't simply give a speech on being creative and then hope it will happen. In fact, 3M's company policy states researchers should spend at least 15 percent of their time on projects they choose. They are also good at sharing technologies across departments and at having management sponsor and support new product development. They have a company structure supporting their goal of creativity.

Organizations are designed with mechanisms to produce stability, and this stability is often confused with "resisting change." This is one of the primary purposes of structure, rules, and hierarchies. They stabilize the organization and make things more predictable. But organizations that desire creativity may have to look at a more organic structure.

Overcoming Resistance to Change: Get it Done!

First, it is important that the people responsible for actually implementing change are at a level in the organization that is high enough to have authority to deal with resistance. Sometimes people do have to be coerced, and if they are not being coerced by someone with authority, the change effort is doomed to fail. Related to that, senior management needs to clearly communicate the need for change in order to get the rest of the organization supportive and committed.

Too often, management does not have a clear vision of what the change is, how it is going to be accomplished, or what the organization should look like after it has changed. A motivational talk about changing for the future and being flexible does not cut it in today's world.

The focus of the change efforts needs to be organization-wide. You can't change one department without affecting the others, yet too often, one department alters procedures or policies or structure without understanding the full scope of the change effort. This results in pushback from the rest of the organization.

If one department decides it is not going along with the change effort, then the whole effort is doomed. The weakest link becomes the point at which the change effort breaks.

Changes in organizations often result in the redistribution of decision-making authority, budgeting, or certain expertise of specialized groups. For example, the introduction of techniques such as participative decision making or self-managed work teams is the kind of change that is often seen as threatening by managers who are used to having full decision authority. The level of disruption that this causes individuals is often underestimated by managers responsible for implementing change.

Leaders need to know what they want, have objective measures in place to evaluate whether they are getting what they want, and reward systems explicitly designed to get the entire organization focused. Managers and employees at all levels need to be rewarded for taking risks, being innovative, and looking for new solutions.

Although each organization is unique, in general this means a flexible, organic structure is best for fostering change. Communication channels need to be open, and this is best accomplished in a flat hierarchy.

Keeping these concepts in mind, what is it that managers change?

Changing Structure

Changing conditions demand structural changes, as discussed in detail in the last chapter. In general, a new structure is needed if the size of the organization has changed. As the organization grows, typically a more complex structure is needed. Competition may dictate the need for a new structure too. Maybe, for example, the organization needs to become more creative. This can be accomplished with a more organic structure.

The key is to recognize this is serious business. Remember that people were attracted to come and work for the organization, in part, because of the structure and the culture that was in place. It is difficult to change that and keep everyone happy. Therefore, success depends on planning these changes up front and involving everyone who is affected.

Changing Culture

I like to consider the culture of the organization as an outcome measure, rather than something that can be changed. I don't like most of the fluffy cultural terms we place on organizations. Statements like, "We need to change the culture around here," don't accomplish anything. Change what you need to change, and the culture will follow.

Starting with culture is like starting to transform a football team by looking at the scoreboard. Yes, we need to score more points, but would you start with the scoreboard? I doubt it. You would look at your quarterback, your receivers, and your offensive line. You would practice harder, bring in new coaches, and train better, for example. Then, come game time, the scoreboard should fix itself.

Even if individuals are open to change, group norms and values are often so solid and so well-established that change is next to impossible. In other words, they may want to change, but the others like things just as they are.

Benjamin Schneider developed the Attraction-Selection-Attrition (ASA) theory that helps explain why this occurs. Individuals are first attracted to a given organization because the job matches their personality. If you like working with people, for instance, you would probably be attracted to an organization that emphasizes sales.

Second, the selection process is designed to make sure you are a fit for the culture. Almost by definition, the selection process seeks out people who would "fit in." In fact, when a person does not get hired because he "wouldn't fit in around here," what does that really mean? I interpret phrases like that to mean that "he wasn't like us." Isn't the selection process heavily oriented toward finding people who fit a certain personality?

Although I may not be attracted to a sales job, maybe the money or other attributes cause me to apply, but I most certainly will not get the job based upon the interview if I am honest. I'm going to say things like, "I don't like talking on the phone," or "Meeting new people is really stressful to me." I shouldn't get the job if the selection process is working.

The final step in the cycle is attrition. This simply means that if I do make it through the interview, I probably won't be around for the long term. I will burn out, not like the job, or be attracted to a different job in a different part of the organization. Schneider says this explains why organizations look the same over the long term.

This theory illustrates both how cultures are developed and how difficult it is to actually bring about change in organizations, especially if the change is going to rock the current status quo. People work for the organization because they like their jobs and they like the culture. To then "change the rules" is incredibly difficult.

Culture changes are much easier in a young organization in which the culture, norms, and rules are still being established. Over time, a stronger culture develops, making change more difficult. In fact, oftentimes, meaningful change cannot be accomplished without "cleaning house" and establishing new rules with different people.

Plus, considering Schneider's framework, changing culture first is next to impossible to do anyway. If, after doing your homework, you determine that a transformation is needed in the culture, be prepared to do this with some new people.

Changing Technology

Technology is changing every industry, even education. I was on the forefront of the online education revolution, as the university had one of the first MBA programs in the nation that was offered totally online. We have a great product, and I'm sold on online education.

I recently saw a demonstration of a software program designed for online education. The blueprints of an office were on the screen. I used my mouse to call meetings, clicked on people I wanted to talk to, and made management decisions using my mouse, all while seeing my "score" at the bottom of the screen.

One time, I reprimanded an employee when I should have been more "sensitive" and, therefore, lost the trust in my team. Fortunately, this was just a simulation, and I rebooted and did it right the second time. I was so engaged that 45 minutes of this just flew by. I got the point of the exercise better than I would have in any other medium.

Prior to this, I thought we were on the cutting edge of technology, and what hit home for me is that in this market, you can only be on the cutting edge for a very short time without retooling and doing it again.

One of my favorite case studies involves an organization that has a proposal on the table for a new piece of chemical mixing equipment that will automate an entire function. The problem is that it will eliminate a department of about 12 people, and these 12 are highly respected in the organization because of their expertise in mixing chemicals. To lose these 12 could demoralize the rest of the organization. People would be thinking that if the organization is not even going to keep the best people around, they surely wouldn't keep me, would they?

On the other hand, technology has eliminated the need for these 12 individuals, and to not buy the technology could result in the entire organization becoming obsolete. Sometimes students propose a solution of buying the technology and keeping the 12 around to run it. If the 12 can be moved to another part of the organization, I would be in favor of it, but I doubt the ROI calculations were made with this type of labor included.

This case study also makes the point that most technological changes involve restructured departments. It is just hard to get around that.

Changing People

What is hard about the previous categories is usually there is not one solid "category" that needs changing. If you change technology, it usually involves changing people and structure too. Therefore, rarely is it only one category that needs changing. All of this goes hand in hand. With most changes, the stress that people go through is similar to the stress people experience with the death of a loved one, or with another major loss in their lives. There are three stages to this:

1. **Shock.** Just like physiological trauma can make our bodies shut down, our minds can shut down and quit processing information. People in shock need common ground among coworkers, and they need information so they can process what is real and what is perceived. Remember, with a lack of information, people will fill in the blanks on their own, thus increasing the level of shock at the pending change.

2. **Defensive retreat.** In trying to maintain the status quo, people will often resort to things like saying, "That's not how we used to do things around here!" It is important to help people realize they don't have to give up everything in order to fit into the new organization. It is also important to listen to what they are saying. Many times, they have keen insights that we ignore, blaming resistance to change.

3. **Acknowledgment.** At this stage, people have finally accepted the change, and should even start to see the positive benefits associated with it.

Change Is NOT Always Good

Now, back to my opening story, six months later:

These sunglasses are a nightmare. The racks look good to start, but we never seem to have the styles that people want. The Convenient Mart wants me to pull all of one style and replace them with another. This will take me about 45 minutes per store, and they have 12 stores. That means two days of labor, including drive time!

I pull all of the sunglasses, order new ones, and then find out that the ones they want are on backorder. Plus, the sunglass company will not refund individual styles, only full racks. I guess there was a misunderstanding. This is a mess! Even though sales are high, profits are only about breaking even; something is wrong. Grandpa was right. We should not have gotten into the sunglasses business.

Later, I made a point to ask Grandpa why he thought the sunglasses would not work. He replied that we are in wholesale distribution. The people who sell sunglasses are in a different industry, and with a different level of expertise. We cannot keep up with what styles sell or what is considered fashionable. He said that even if a company guarantees that they will accept returns on products that don't sell, the labor and the paperwork are a nightmare, and we don't get our refunds until about 90 days after we return them.

Finally, he said that he had a similar experience with sunglasses 30 years ago, and that is how he knew all of this! I wondered why he didn't tell us all of this ahead of time. I guess he just thought we would do what we wanted anyway.

The academic models on the topic of change tend to begin with the assumption that change is in fact needed, and when it is not happening, it must be because people are resisting change. I would posit that it is not change itself that people resist, but rather the potential negative impact that the change could bring. There is a difference.

Consider the example discussed previously in which I stated that students tend to sit in the same chairs in classrooms. Asking them to switch makes them uncomfortable. While this may illustrate in part some psychological phenomenon, further examination illustrates that this behavior is, in fact, totally rational. Consider the actual reasons why you sit where you sit in a classroom, a meeting, or in church.

I prefer a seat where I can make a clean exit should I need to get out of the room. I also like lots of space around me to spread out, and I like to be able to see everyone at one time. This generally puts me in the back corner of a room, which is what I like. I don't like the front row, as I have to turn around to see the rest of the group, and I don't like sitting in the middle of a row, because there is generally less space, and I can't get out.

In every group, there are participants who like to sit in the front row. It could be that, for them, they can see better, hear better, or block out distractions. So, of course, if I swapped seats with a person who liked the front row, we both would be uncomfortable. But our discomfort is for real reasons, not for some deep-seated psychological phenomenon.

It is not change itself that people resist, but rather the negative impact of the change. It is not always fair to brand people as "change resistors" when they have real reasons for not wanting to change.

In this case, my grandfather was not resisting change per se because he had several logical reasons why we should not sell sunglasses. Had he been active in the business, branding him as a typical change resistor would cause us not to listen to his arguments, thus causing the organization to make a bad decision.

So don't automatically assume that those resisting change are wrong. Sometimes they have good ideas that don't get on the table because of the assumption that they are just "resisting change."

This does not contradict or go against the concepts discussed in this chapter. It simply points out that leaders need to listen to the ideas of others before branding them as change resistors.

Accelerating Change
through Effective Leadership

This book does not directly deal with the study of leadership. A large body of literature examines what makes an effective leader, what traits leaders share in common and which styles are most effective in certain situations. This is good literature, but simply beyond the scope of this book. However, I do want to touch on two key concepts that have really affected how I look at the concept of improving an organization.

Employee Engagement

Research conducted by The Gallup Organization has shown that the best organizations do things differently when it comes to creating what they call "engaged customers." The best organizations understand the key to long-term survival is to have customers who are emotionally attached to the organization. Customers who shop your location because of price or convenience are unstable because they will leave without a second thought if a cheaper price or a more convenient location opens. An engaged customer does business with you because of the way it makes them feel, and this is a stable customer.

To create an engaged customer base, you need engaged employees. These are the employees who also have an attachment to the organization well beyond a paycheck, or even beyond simply being satisfied with their jobs. Engaged employees are particularly in tune with what the customers want and have the desire, motivation, and tools to create customers who consistently return to your location because of the way it makes them feel.

Creating an engaged team begins with understanding that each person has his or her own unique talents and abilities, and it is much easier to work with those talents rather than take the "hire first, train later" approach. So many training initiatives fail because they focus on fixing weaknesses. Per Chapter 2, the focus tends to be on creating new paths in people, instead of using the paths that already exist.

Gallup has instruments that measure other aspects of engagement, such as how the team views the mission of the organization, the quality of management feedback, and whether or not the employees have the tools to do the job properly. This is a framework that will help organizations through change, because it encompasses so many aspects of management. Gallup knows that the world's best organizations do things differently than the others.

Authentic Leadership

Authentic leadership has as its basic premise that people are the most effective when they are true to themselves and to others. This is accomplished by owning your own personal experiences and understanding who you are. Second, authentic leaders act in accordance with who they really are. People are "transparent" when you can see right

> *You can't build a reputation on what you are going to do.*
>
> Henry Ford

through them in a positive sense—what they do is who they are with no hidden agendas or actions.

A large part of authentic leadership is the trust and honesty that a leader portrays. It is hard to successfully lead a change effort, or to get people to do anything your way, for that manner, if they do not trust you. Mutual trust is important. Without it, you have nothing.

Dale, one of our veteran sales staff, pulled me aside after the sales meeting. It seems as if he saw something suspicious about one of the delivery drivers, Larry, as he was pulling into the parking lot. Dale saw Larry run to his car, unlock it, toss something in the back seat, then go back inside.

Please don't tell me he is stealing, he is really a hard worker. Plus, I just got the warehouse fully staffed again, and I don't want to deal with this. Well, this is easy, I'll just go tell Larry what I heard, ask to see the back seat of his car, and clear up this misunderstanding.

I asked Larry about the incident. At first, he couldn't remember running to the car, then he quickly stated, "Oh, yeah! I did purchase two boxes of Hershey Bars. I just hadn't gotten up to the front counter to pay for them yet."

Dammit! I wished he had stuck with his denial. Now, I have a gray area. As a very careful decision maker, I tell him that I don't really know what to do, but I will let him know by the end of the day. My sources were split on the issue. Dale is convinced that there is no way an employee would run that fast to his car if he intended on paying. Dad says I should let him go; there are plenty of other good workers to be found.

I'm sitting in my office staring into space when Larry comes into my office crying, saying he needs this job, he has a family to support, and that I can't fire him because of his simple mistake of not making it to the front counter yet. I err on the side of caution, figuring I can always fire him later if I choose—after all, he was crying in my office.

As you guessed, it was, in fact, the wrong decision. I never believed that he was innocent, and we were always uncomfortable around each other. I felt that the rest of the team thought I let him get away with a crime, and I lost some of their respect because of that. I never gave him any additional responsibilities and never let him be alone in any part of the warehouse.

The final straw came when I saw him eating a product that we sell for lunch. I asked him if he paid for it, to which he replied that he got it from the grocery store. I stopped short of asking him for a receipt, but we could both tell that it was over. He ended up quitting later that year.

The lesson is that relationships require mutual trust and honesty to be viable. If I don't trust the salesperson at the clothing store, the mechanic who works on my car, or my children to tell me the truth, the relationship is damaged. I didn't trust Larry; therefore, I wouldn't give him any meaningful projects. He saw that, and his work performance deteriorated too. After all, how much fun is it to work for a boss who thinks you are a thief?

People like following effective leaders and will imitate and copy leader behaviors. The old adage, "Do as I say, not as I do," does not work in the leadership arena. If I want my team to work hard on Friday afternoons, I need to work hard on Friday afternoons too. I can't make that my golf day, and then wonder why my team is not as productive on Fridays as they should be.

I was with a business owner many years ago, and we were touring several of his retail convenience stores. At one location, he took a couple of packs of cigarettes for himself and told the store manager what he was doing. He then confided in me later that he thought this store manager was stealing from him and was trying to figure out what to do about it. Yes, a business owner has the right, I suppose, to take product if he wishes. But he was sending the signal that it is OK to steal "just a little bit."

Contrast this to another restaurant owner who invited me to his restaurant for lunch. When the check came, he paid the waitress in cash. I expected him to initial the check or something, but to pay cash did initially surprise me. Then I realized what signal he was sending by doing this: Everyone pays, including the owner! What a lesson in leadership.

Looking to the Future

I would like to close this book with a final case study:

A powerful, charismatic leader is having problems. A well-known consultant is called in to help. The consultant notices that the leader tries to handle all problems and conflicts among his people himself. People tend to line up in front of his office. Because the leader is overwhelmed, he cannot handle all the business.

So the consultant has a conversation with the leader and tells him to structure his organization by delegating authority and empowering subordinates to handle more of the workload. These subordinates should be selected not only on their leadership abilities but also on their character. They should be truthful, not driven by money. The new structure should resolve all daily issues at the lowest possible level; only the big and difficult issues should be brought before the leader.

He should focus on strategy, on dealing with top management, on establishing new approaches, and on teaching these skills to the people, showing them the way to go and the work to be done. The case study states that the leader listens to the consultant and carries out the reorganization, which is a success, and the consultant returns home.

This is a short case study that I use in class and in seminars. I like to ask participants where they think this case study originated. Many of them say it sounds like the organization in which they work, or that they read something similar in a business magazine recently.

This case study actually is a slightly modified version of a story from the Bible. You can see the full original story in Exodus 18:13-27. The charismatic leader is Moses, who is in the process of leading his people from Egypt to Palestine. The consultant is Jethro, Moses' father-in-law. They were discussing many management issues, including delegation, empowerment, employee selection, character in leadership, strategic planning, and job design.

What is interesting is that this was written over 3,000 years ago, and we are still dealing with the same management issues today! The interesting thing about managing people is that we probably will always be dealing with the same issues. The challenge, then, is to continue to harness new research and continually improve, without trying to make it perfect. It never will be perfect; we can only try to make things a little bit better.

That is why I was so comfortable with putting my story, my mistakes, and my experiences in this book. I know that you are experiencing similar challenges, regardless of your industry. Technology is changing rapidly; people, on the other hand, are not. Therefore, the best thing you can do as a manager is to recognize that people are different, they all have their shortcomings, and things will never be perfect. Our challenge, therefore, is to do the best we can, while enjoying the ride along the way!

Summary of Key Points

- While the topic of change has been studied for decades, the speed of change in today's organizations is creating many new management challenges.
- Lewin's classic model proposed that, for real change to occur, either forces for change needed to increase or resistance to change needed to decrease.
- Although individuals do resist change, it is often for a very good reason and not due to some psychological phenomenon that humans have.
- The system itself is often the source of resistance, and many times, this resistance is intentionally built into the system.
- Managers can change the structure, culture, technology, or people.
- Engaged workers are those that participate in the organization because they have an emotional attachment to it. This in turn creates engaged customers, which are needed for long-term survival in today's economy.
- Authentic leaders are leaders who are true to themselves, and open and honest with those with whom they work.
- When managing people, almost all of us are facing the same challenging issues.

Selected References

Details on the various waves and revolutions that have transpired in our economy can be found at A. Toffler, *The Third Wave* (New York: Bantam Books, 1984).

For details on the "triple convergence," see the best-selling book by T. Friedman, *The World Is Flat: A Brief History of the Twenty-First Century* (New York: Farrar, Straus, and Giroux, 2005).

For details on the classic force-field model of change, see K. Lewin, *Field-Theory in Social Science* (New York: Harper and Row, 1951).

The statistics about technology penetrating 30 percent of U.S. households is discussed in M. Echols, *Competitive Advantage from Human Capital Investment* (Arlington, TX: Tapestry Press, 2006).

Details about the Attraction-Selection-Attrition model are at B. Schneider, H. Goldstein, and D. Smith, "The ASA Framework: An Update," *Personnel Psychology*, Vol. 48 (1995), pp. 747-773.

The Gallup Organization's concept of engagement is detailed at C. Coffman and G. Gonzales-Molina, *Follow This Path: How the World's Greatest Organizations Drive Growth by Unleashing Human Potential* (New York: Warner Books, 2002).

The concept of authentic leadership is detailed at B. Avolio, W. Gardner, F. Walumbwa, F. Luthans, and D. May, "Unlocking the Mask: A Look at the Process by Which Authentic Leaders Impact Follower Attitudes and Behaviors," *The Leadership Quarterly*, Vol. 15 (2004), pp. 801-823.

The case study at the end of this chapter is adapted from F. Luthans, *Organizational Behavior* (New York: McGraw Hill, 2005).

The quotations by Patricia Fripp & Arthur Fripp in Chapters 4-6 are from Patricia Fripp's book, *Make It, So You Don't Have to Fake It!* (Mechanicsburg, PA: Executive Books, 1999).

Several of the quotes throughout this book are from P. McWilliams book, *Do It! Let's Get Off Our Buts* (Los Angeles: Prelude Press, 1994).

Index

N

O

Details on My Work
at Farner-Bocken Company

Many of the stories in the book originated from the time I worked in our family's business, Farner-Bocken Company. This was founded by my Grandfather and his partner, Don Bocken, in 1939. The company is a wholesale distributer of candy, groceries, paper products, and foodservice items. Customers include large convenience store chains, restaurants, concession stands, taverns, and grocery stores.

In Chapter 2, I was filling in for a salesman who was on vacation, which meant going to the customer's location once a week. A typical convenience store customer would allow our salespeople to do most of the ordering. This involved walking each aisle and ordering needed items, pulling old products from the shelf, and merchandising the store for maximum sales. After ordering, we would sit down with the store manager and show them new items, special deals, and suggest ways that they could increase their sales.

At the end of the day, these orders were entered into our computer and processed at one of our 10 locations. The night shift would print out the orders, process them, and then load them onto the trucks. This process was somewhat complex due to the fact that there were over 14,000 line items and a wide variety of product types (such as frozen foods, refrigerated produce, canned items, candy, etc.).

They were then delivered the next morning. I recall anxiously awaiting my 16th birthday so that I could become a delivery driver and get out of the warehouse. It was an important job, because drivers were the only ones besides the salesperson who were in regular contact with the customer. The orders could be quite large, so this job oftentimes involved putting the order away in the proper location and handling any problems, such as writing credits for damaged products or fixing mistakes in ordering.

In Chapter 4, I made reference to the delivery drivers helping out in the warehouse once they finished their deliveries. This was in reference to a host of things that have to happen in order to get the system ready for the next round of orders. This included such things as ordering inventory, receiving products, stocking shelves, and making boxes to pack the next night's orders in. It also involved general maintenance activities, such as sweeping the floor or washing the trucks.

I was fortunate to be involved in all areas of the business. I worked on the night shift, managed delivery drivers, had a sales route, managed a sales team, and attended a board meeting. This really gave me a well-rounded perspective on what managers face at all levels of the organization.

About the Author

Steve Farner's journey into management began many years ago when he decided to quit attending his principles of management course in college because it was, in his view, "common sense." He changed his major to finance and graduated from Iowa State University. He then transferred to a branch location in his family's candy and grocery wholesale distribution business, Farner-Bocken Company, where he worked for the next eight years.

During this time, he pursued his MBA at Creighton University. The management concepts and theories that he studied showed him the enormous potential of people who are both motivated and have the ability to produce at their best, and he decided that he wanted a career studying and espousing these principles.

He received his Ph.D. in Management from the University of Nebraska, Lincoln. His main interest is organizational behavior, which emphasizes the psychological side of what makes people do what they do.

Steve teaches management courses to graduate and undergraduate students, online and in the classroom, at both Bellevue University and the University of Nebraska. He also develops and delivers customized management programs for specific organizations, both for classroom and online delivery.

He has published articles on the topics of customer service, 360-degree performance appraisal, and the effects of motivated, engaged employees on customers. His other writing projects include reviewing management texts and writing instructors' manuals for companies such as McGraw-Hill and Prentice Hall.

He was prompted to write this book because of the overwhelmingly positive response he received from his keynote talks and management programs. Managers and employees alike can relate to the stories he tells and find application in their own careers.

ORDER COPIES FOR YOUR STAFF!

Customer Name: _____

Date: _____

Shipping Address:_____

City:_____ State: _____ Zip:_____

Telephone: (___) _____

Email: _____

Price: $29.95 x _____(number of copies)　　　$ _____

Sales Tax (7% when shipped to Nebraska addresses only) $ _____

Shipping Costs: $4.00 for 1ˢᵗ book (allow 2 weeks)

$1.50 for each additional book $ _____

TOTAL $ _____

PAYMENT METHOD:

☐ Check enclosed made payable to "Farner Group"

☐ VISA ☐ MasterCard ☐ American Express ☐ Discover

Name on Card: _____

Billing Address (if different from above) _____

Account Number: _____

CVV _____ Exp. Date_____

(3 digits on back of card near signature on Visa/MC/Discover - 4 digits on front of AmEx)

Cardholder's Signature: _____

MAIL THIS FORM TO:

Farner Group
P.O. Box 642313
Omaha, Nebraska 68164

Or order online at: *www.SteveFarner.com*

Want to learn more?

I'm available to speak to your organization or managers today. I conduct workshops, keynote talks, and leadership programs for organizations and for conferences and conventions. If you are looking for a speaker for your next event, contact me. I'll share insightful managerial tales and tips, including how to educate people at all levels of the organization on how to better work together, and help them understand why correctly managing and leading people is critical for the long-term success of any organization.

For more information and availability, visit *www.SteveFarner.com*.

Comments from Previous Workshop Attendees and Former Students

"This webinar was excellent. Thank you for getting to and sticking with the topic. Great job!!"

"…While clearly having an academic focus, Dr. Farner was very in tune with challenges in the field."

"Extremely knowledgeable and made very strong points."

"Steve's thoughts on return on investment resonated with my financial thinking and offered thoughts on how best to 'quantify' the value of learning interventions."